# CARDINAL NEWMAN

## TROJAN HORSE
## IN THE CHURCH

by

Reverend Paul M. Kimball

DOLOROSA PRESS
Camillus, New York
2019

CARDINAL NEWMAN:
TROJAN HORSE IN THE CHURCH

ISBN: 978-1-7327175-6-5

To order additional copies, please contact:

## DOLOROSA PRESS
**www.dolorosapress.com**

**Email: avemaria@dolorosapress.com**

# *Contents*

# Introduction

Cardinal Newman is an enigma. By traditional Catholics he is touted as an anti-Liberal, while liberal Catholics hail him as the "Father of the Second Vatican Council." During his lifetime his writings were highly controversial, but now one would be attacked on both sides for finding any fault with them. As Father Joseph Clifford Fenton wrote: "Newman has suffered what is for him the supreme indignity of becoming fashionable. Far more indiscriminate praise than really critical study has been given to his writings. Modern Catholic literature has tended to make a hero out of Newman and has endeavored to justify rather than to explain his contentions."[1] Orestes Brownson when critiquing Newman's writings soon after they were written lamented that already in his time, "There is a decided tendency to abandon the scholastic method for the rhetorical."[2] He anticipated that anyone who dared to criticize Cardinal Newman would be exposing himself "to much misconstruction and odium," but nevertheless rightly offers his neck to the sword. For as he bravely wrote, 'Personal considerations must not be suffered to enter into the account. The man, who, when the purity and integrity of the Catholic faith is attacked by an insidious theory, will remain silent lest his own motives should be miscon-

---

1 For every critical and discriminating study like Dr. Bernard's *A Preface to Newman's Theology* there are a half dozen works which becloud the ideas of Newman through their very anxiety to eulogize him. Monsignor Joseph Clifford Fenton, "John Henry Newman and the Vatican Definition of Papal Infallibility," *The American Ecclesiastical Review*, vol. 113, n. 4 (October 1945), p. 300.

2 Orestes Brownson, "Newman's Theory of Christian Doctrine," *Brownson's Quarterly Review*, vol. 1 (January, 1847), p. 85.

strued, or offer an apology for speaking out in clear and energetic tones against the advancing error, has little reason to glory in his Catholicity."[3]

That Cardinal Newman was controversial in his own day was recalled ten years ago in *L'Osservatore Romano*: "It was the Second Vatican Council, of which he is often called 'the Father,' that finally vindicated his theology. The late Cardinal Avery Dulles called him the most seminal Catholic theologian of the 19th century. His classic *Essay on the Development of Christian Doctrine* (1845), which fell under the suspicion of the two leading Roman theologians of the day, is the starting-point for modern Catholic theology of development. His *On Consulting the Faithful in Matters of Doctrine* (1859), which was denounced to Rome by one of the English and Welsh hierarchy, predated by more than a hundred years the Second Vatican Council's Decree on the Apostolate of the Laity and the chapter on the laity in the Constitution on the Church. The final chapter of the latter on the Blessed Virgin Mary was the result of the Council's decision not to have a separate document on Our Lady; its Scriptural and Patristic theology is in accord with Newman's own Mariology in his *A Letter to Pusey* (1866). Newman's interpretation of the First Vatican Council's definition of papal infallibility in his *Letter to the Duke of Norfolk* (1875) was unwelcome to the extreme Ultramontanes..."[4]

Alec Vidler, an Anglican historian held that Newman was not strictly a modernist but was merely used as a shield by the Modernists:

---

3 *Ibid.* p. 84.
4 Ian Ker, "The Father of Vatican II," <u>L'Osservatore Romano</u>, July 22, 2009, page 7.

Newman is often described as a precursor, even as the only precursor, of Modernism.[5] The amount of truth in this description is strictly limited. No doubt he was the only nineteenth-century theologian whom the modernists found useful. But they found him useful, not because he was by any means the most liberal, or progressive, or distinctively modern, theologian that the Roman Church produced in the nineteenth century, but because he had been more liberal than any other theologian whose name was held in honor in official circles. This was not so, of course, during the pontificate of Pius IX, although even then the fact that Newman was the greatest asset that the Roman Church in England possessed kept the official hostility to him respectful. It was the conferring on him by Leo XIII of a cardinal's hat (in 1879) that gave to his name a singular prestige both within and without the Church and to his writings an implied authoritative approval which they would not otherwise have had...

So indeed it seemed, and so it may have been—for the time being. But by a curious irony it was chiefly because Newman had been made a cardinal that during the modernist movement he was signaled out as the most advanced liberal Catholic theologian of his generation, while the genuine liberals, such as the 'Rambler' writers, who approached far more nearly to

---

5 E.g. 'Dans tous les pays d'Europe où le Modernisme s'etait implanté et propagé, l'Angleterre était le seul où le mouvement, dans son contenu essentiel: apologétique et histoire du dogme, pût compter un précurseur, veritable et caractéristique' ['In all the countries of Europe where Modernism was implanted and propagated, England was the only one where movement, in its essential content: apologetics and the history of dogma, could count a precursor, true and characteristic.'] (E. Buonaiuti, *Le Modernisme catholique* (1927), p. 130).

an anticipation of Modernism than Newman ever did, were overlooked. For the modernists to have recalled *their* work would have been to invite trouble, and they had trouble enough as it was; on the other hand, to invoke the authority of the illustrious cardinal was not only safe, but—in a Church where great store is set on precedents—invaluable.[6]

Now when Pope Saint Pius X condemned Modernism in his encyclical *Pascendi* in 1907, many, including his official biographer and long-time friend, Wilfrid Ward, assumed that Cardinal Newman's ideas, such as his theory of the development of doctrine was included in the condemnation.

For the next four years Rome selectively built her case against the various modernists, and in the summer of 1907 issued the condemnations of their lives and works in *Lamentabili* and *Pascendi dominici gregis*. On the face of both documents, various of Newman's ideas, contained primarily in the *Essay on Development, On Consulting the Faithful in Matters of Doctrine*, and the *Grammar of Assent*, would seem to have been condemned implicitly, if not in explicit intention. Most of the modernists thought it so, and many antimodernists feared it might be so as well. Consequently, a public debate on whether or not Newman was condemned by the papal documents ensued.[7] The antimodernists in England, especially the Oratorians, the Benedictine Francis Aidan Gasquet (soon to be Cardinal Gasquet), and the diocesan theologian for Westminster, Canon James Moyes, argued in a merely extrinsic way that Newman was not condemned because the pope and

---

6 *The Modernist Movement in the Catholic Church: Its Origins & Outcome*, pp. 51-52.

7 For a discussion of this issue, see Barmann, *Baron Friedrich von Hügel*, pp. 20-46.

his secretary of state said that he was not. After all, for one pope to make a man a cardinal and for his successor to declare the same man a heretic was not the Roman manner. The modernists, on the other hand, argued from a comparison based on a theological understanding of what Newman actually wrote with what the encyclical said was unacceptable ecclesiastically. And these latter concluded that Newman had indeed been condemned by the letter of the documents, even if not by the actual intention of their authors. Wilfrid Ward, who had already been appointed Newman's official biographer and who knew Newman's works better, perhaps, than anyone at the time, was a friend of von Hügel and Tyrrell, and was familiar with Loisy's work as well. Ward was convinced that Newman had been condemned by *Pascendi* and wrote to Father John Norris of the Birmingham Oratory: 'Gasquet had ridiculed the idea that the Encyclical hit J.H.N., but as I told Norfolk three weeks ago it not only hits him but the analysis of Modernism includes all on which his heart was set for 40 years and brands it as false and absurd.... we cannot defend him successfully without going in the teeth of the Encyclical, which brands also positions essential to his views... I think the situation simply tragic.'[8] Two days after Ward wrote that letter, Norris placed a letter of his own in the *London Times* which said, "I am enabled to state on information received today from the highest authority that the 'genuine doctrine and spirit of Newman's Catholic teaching are not hit by the Encyclical, but the theories of many who wrongly seek refuge

---

8 Wilfrid Ward to John Norris, November 2, 1907, in Edward E. Kelly, "Newman, Wilfrid Ward, and the Modernist Crisis," *Thought* XLII (Winter 1973): p. 515.

under a great name are obviously censured."'[9] Apparently that was all Ward wanted, for he wrote to Norris the same day: *"Deo Gratias. I simply cannot express the relief I felt when I read your letter in the 'Times' and the words you quote."*[10] Several weeks earlier Ward had suggested to von Hügel a plan for getting Church authorities publicly to discriminate between those condemned by *Pascendi* and ideas of Newman which seemed to many to be very like those of the condemned modernists. Von Hügel thought the idea a bad one because it would be agreeing to the destruction of men and ideas also important to the Church in order to save Newman. "Even at this moment they may shrink from publicly admitting that Newman was also aimed at," von Hügel told Ward," ... but I am certain they as little like J.H.N. as they like you or me."[11]

Consequently, the next year, Pius X felt obliged to publicly defend Cardinal Newman by writing a letter of approval of a book exonerating Newman of the allegation of being a modernist entitled, *Cardinal Newman and the Encyclical Pascendi Dominici Gregis.*[12] In it the pope wrote: "Venerable Brother, greetings and Our Apostolic blessing. We hereby inform you that your essay, in which you show that the writings of Cardinal

9 *The Times*, no. 38,481 (November 4, 1907).

10 Wilfrid Ward to John Norris, November 4, 1907, in Maisie Ward, *Insurrection*, p. 269.

11 Friedrich von Hügel to Wilfrid Ward, October 18, 1907, in Barmann, *Baron Friedrich von Hügel*, p. 205; Lawrence Barmann, "Theological Inquiry in an Authoritarian Church: Newman and Modernism," in *Discourse and Context : An Interdisciplinary Study of John Henry Newman*, ed. by Gerard Magill (Carbondale, Southern Illinois University Press, 1993), pp. 184-186.

12 Edward Thomas O'Dwyer, Bishop of Limerick, *Cardinal Newman and the encyclical Pascendi dominici gregis: an essay* (London, Longmans, Green and Co., 1908).

Newman, far from being in disagreement with Our Encyclical Letter *Pascendi*, are very much in harmony with it, has been emphatically approved by Us: for you could not have better served both the truth and the dignity of man."[13] It is curious that the pope equated defending Cardinal Newman with serving "the dignity of man," for in his letter to *Le Sillon*, written two years later, he wrote: "[The Sillonists] have a particular conception of *human dignity*, freedom, justice and brotherhood; and, in an attempt to justify their social dreams, they put forward the Gospel."[14] Now since the pope had warned in *Pascendi* that "... the danger is present almost in the very veins and heart of the Church,"[15] could it be that one of his secretaries who composed this letter inserted a mischievous phase?

The effect of Pius X's support of Newman can be seen in a *volte-face* of Rev. Dr. William Francis Barry. For in 1903 he had written in his biography of Newman:

Born in the City of London, not far from the Bank, on February 21, 1801, John Henry was the son of John Newman and Jemima Fourdrinier his wife, the eldest of six children, three boys and three girls. "His father," says Thomas Mozley, "was of a family of small landed proprietors in Cambridgeshire, and had an hereditary taste for music, of which he had a practical and scientific knowledge, together with much general culture." He was chief clerk and afterwards partner in a banking firm, was also a Freemason, with a high standing in the craft, an admirer of Franklin and an

---

13 Letter of March 10, 1908: In which Pope Pius X approves the work of the Bishop of Limerick on the writings of Cardinal Newman. To Bishop Edward Thomas O'Dwyer of Limerick, *Acta Sanctae Sedis*, vol. 41, 1908.

14 Pope Pius X – 1910, "Our Apostolic Mandate."

15 *Pascendi*, n. 3.

enthusiastic reader of Shakespeare. These particulars, except the last, will prepare us for the fact that in an earlier generation the family had spelt its signature "Newmann"; that it was understood to be of Dutch origin; and that its real descent was Hebrew. The talent for music, calculation, and business, the untiring energy, legal acumen, and dislike of speculative metaphysics, which were conspicuous in John Henry, bear out this interesting genealogy. A large part of his character and writings will become intelligible if we keep it in mind. That his features had a strong Jewish cast, is evident from his portraits, and was especially to be noted in old age. It may be conjectured that the migration of these Dutch Jews to England fell within a period not very distant from the death of Spinoza in 1675.[16]

But in 1911, when chosen to write the article in the *Catholic Encyclopedia* about Newman, Barry undermined what he himself had previously wrote, saying: "…the suggestion has been thrown out that to his Hebrew affinities the cardinal owed, not only the cast of his features, but some of his decided characteristics—e. g., his remarkable skill in music and mathematics, his dislike of metaphysical speculations, his grasp of the concrete, and his nervous temperament. But no documentary evidence has been found to confirm the suggestion."[17]

Even if Cardinal Newman has been exonerated from charges of Modernism, should he now be raised up to the altars as recently announced for October 13, 2019? On July 3, 2009, Pope Benedict XVI recognized the

---

16 William Francis Barry, *Newman* (London, Hodder and Stoughton, 1904), pp. 8-10.

17 Barry, William. "John Henry Newman," *The Catholic Encyclopedia* (New York: Robert Appleton Company, 1911), vol. 10, p. 794.

healing of Deacon Jack Sullivan in 2001 as a miracle for Newman's beatification, which occurred on September 19, 2010. Now Mr. Sullivan underwent the operation of "... a laminectomy to remove a part of the spinal bones that was causing the problem... Although successfully performed in August 2001, this operation left Jack Sullivan in immense pain and he was warned a full recovery might take months. With the new term approaching, Mr. Sullivan was becoming increasingly anxious about returning to class, and just a few days after his operation he tried to get out of bed. Having taken an excruciating few minutes, with a nurse's help, to get his feet to the floor, he said he leant on his forearms and recited his prayer to Newman. Michael Powell, a consultant neurosurgeon at London's University College Hospital, said a typical laminectomy took 'about 40 minutes, and most patients... walk out happy at two days.'"[18] Furthermore, the directive *De Canonizatione* of Prospero Cardinal Lambertini, who was later crowned Pope Benedict XIV, spelt out the rules for working out if a healing was really a miracle from heaven. It is astounding that this miracle has been approved, for it directly violates the third rule of Benedict XIV for the verification of miracles during the process of canonization of saints, namely, "The patient should not be getting medical treatment around the time of the cure."

Earlier this year, on February 13, 2019, it was announced that Pope Francis had approved the Decree concerning the second miracle required for Newman's canonization. It is said to have happened to a woman who started to hemorrhage and locked herself in the bathroom. She felt she was losing her baby. At that moment she called out, "Cardinal Newman, please

---

18 Michael Hirst, "Papal visit: Cardinal Newman's 'miracle cure'," BBC News, September 13, 2010.

stop the bleeding!" The bleeding immediately stopped. However, at no point were doctors asked if a miracle occurred. They only had to answer if there was any known medical explanation for what happened. But this seems to violate another rule of Pope Benedict XIV, namely the sixth: "The cure must not come at a time when some natural cause could make the patient think he is cured or which simulates a cure."[19]

---

19 *Doctrina de servorum Dei beatificatione et beatorum canonizatione*, lib. 4, p. 1, c. 7, n. 1-2.

# I

## *Personal Character*

The devil's advocate of the beatification process, whose role was sadly eliminated by Pope John Paul II in 1983, certainly ought to raise the question of Newman's close relationship with Fr. Ambrose St. John. In Newman's private chapel on a side wall near the altar are framed photographs of his close friends, among which Ambrose's photo is larger than others. Both were strangely buried together. "[Newman] died on the 11th of August 1890, in his ninetieth year, and was buried, by his own request, in the same grave with his friend Ambrose St. John."[20] In 2008, however, the Vatican ordered that Fr. Ambrose St. John's remains be separated from those of Newman, contrary to Newman's dying wishes, in preparation for Newman's possible canonization.

Likewise, soon before Fr. Ambrose died, Newman was completely distraught.

Albany Christie walked with him from Oxford to Littlemore when the great separation of 1845 was approaching. Newman never spoke a word all the way, and Christie's hand when they arrived was wet with Newman's tears. When he made his confession in Littlemore chapel his exhaustion was such that he could not walk without help. When he went to Rome to set right the differences with his brethren of London which tried him so deeply, he walked barefoot from the halting stage of the diligence all the way to St. Peter's Basilica. When Ambrose St. John died Newman

---

20 "Cardinal Newman," *Edinburgh Review*, vol. 215, n. 440 (April, 1912), p. 271.

threw himself on the bed by the corpse and spent the night there.[21]

Wilfrid Ward is the principal witness of this strange reaction. "According to Newman's first biographer, Wilfrid Ward, who knew both men, and may have gotten the information from Newman himself: 'Newman [indeed] threw himself on the bed by the corpse and spent the night there.' This has been challenged by subsequent biographers. What is not in dispute is that, according to the reliable William Neville, Newman said the Office for the dead that night, wrote telegrams and letters, and in the early hours celebrated Mass for his deceased friend."[22] For example, one of Newman's more recent biographers, Charles Stephen Dessain, "…claims there is 'no warrant' for Ward's assertion that 'when Ambrose St. John died Newman threw himself on the bed by the corpse and spent the night there.'[23] But Dessain's account of Newman's actions that night does not nullify Ward's account. Moreover, Newman's uninhibited expression of his grief in letters after the death confirms the possibility of Ward's account.[24] Ward apparently learned of Newman's expression of grief from some Oratorian: perhaps from Dennis Sheil who remembered Newman's bursting into tears when he came to give absolution at the burial service of St. John."[25]

---

21 Ward, I, pp. 21-22.

22 Ian Ker, *John Henry Newman: A Biography* (Oxford, Oxford University Press, 2009), p. 694; John Cornwell, *Newman's Unquiet Grave: The Reluctant Saint* (New York, A&C Black, 2011), p. 205

23 Charles Stephen Dessain, *Letters and Diaries* XXVII, p. 301, and Ward, I, pp. 21-22.

24 See Dessain, XXVII, pp. 301-320, especially 306.

25 Reverend Edward E. Kelly, "Newman's Reputation and the Biographical Tradition," *Faith & Reason*, vol. 15, n. 4 (winter, 1989), p. 5. Reverend Edward E. Kelly received his doctorate in English from Fordham University. A successful teacher and writer, he

# II
## *Ambiguity*

But it is less important to study the personal character of Newman than to properly plumb the depth of Newman's orthodoxy. In this analysis of his orthodoxy, neither the approval of a saintly pontiff nor miraculous cures override the divinely given test preached by Saint Paul: "But though we, or an angel from heaven, preach a gospel to you besides that which we have preached to you, let him be anathema."[26] Admittedly Newman was submissive to Church authority and not a heretic, and the content of his teaching was declared by Pope Pius X not to be modernistic. Still the theories that he devised while being a Protestant for development of Catholic doctrine are certainly suspect. But his teachings are neither clear nor consistent, as shall be shown below. The chief difficulty in analyzing the teachings of Cardinal Newman, then, will be his elusive presentation of his own thoughts, most likely so presented to avoid being censured by the Catholic hierarchy.

Firstly, Newman's writings are often ambiguous about the necessity of membership in the Catholic Church. For Msgr. Talbot, Chamberlain to Pope Pius IX, wrote in a letter to Archbishop Manning of Westminster, "Newman's work none here can understand. Poor man, by living almost ever since he has been a

---

is at present Professor of English at St. Louis University. Father Kelly worked with the late C. Stephen Dessain in the Newman archives at the Oratory in Birmingham, England. He has also edited a volume of Newman's letters and has published articles on Newman and other modern literary figures. This is reported by Vincent Blehl, "The Sanctity of Cardinal Newman," *America,* 1958.

26 Gal. 1, 8.

Catholic surrounded by a set of inferior men who idolize him, I do not think he has ever acquired the Catholic instincts. I have reason to suppose that secretly he has always sympathized with the *Rambler* school... I know that the Anglicans look on the *Apologia* as a plea for remaining as they are. What makes this more anxious is that there is the same school growing up in France."[27]

Secondly, Newman was ambiguous when speaking about the content of the deposit of the faith, as later done by modernists who lived after him.

The controversy over this point may easily become a mere logomachy; the writings of the Modernists are sometimes as capable of double interpretation as are the words of Newman. For example, these words of Loisy, if taken entirely apart from the light which Loisy's critical work throws upon their meaning, might be given an interpretation in harmony with either of the interpretations which have been made of Newman's theory: "The conceptions that the church presents as revealed dogmas are not truths fallen from heaven, and preserved by religious traditions in the precise form in which they first appeared. The historian sees in them the interpretation of religious facts, acquired by a laborious effort of theological thought. Though the dogmas may be divine in origin and substance, they are human in structure and composition."[28]

Such ambivalence of modernists was noted by Pope Pius X in his encyclical *Pascendi*: "This becomes still clearer to anybody who studies the conduct of

---

27 Letter of Msgr. Talbot to Archbishop Manning, February 25, 1866 in Edmund Sheridan Purcell, *Life of Cardinal Manning, Archbishop of Westminster*, vol. 2, p. 323.

28 Loisy, *The Gospel and the Church*, p. 210; William Henry Allison, "Was Newman a Modernist?", *The American Journal of Theology*, Vol. 14, n. 4 (Oct. 1910), p. 566.

Modernists, which is in perfect harmony with their teachings. In the writings and addresses they seem not infrequently to advocate now one doctrine now another so that one would be disposed to regard them as vague and doubtful. But there is a reason for this, and it is to be found in their ideas as to the mutual separation of science and faith. Hence in their books you find some things which might well be expressed by a Catholic, but in the next page you find other things which might have been dictated by a rationalist."[29]

Thirdly, Newman's teaching about whether the Apostles were infallible is inconsistent, perhaps because he also held that doctrine could be viewed by science and history differently than by the light of faith. For example he wrote, "For since, as all allow, the Apostles were infallible, it tells against their infallibility, or the infallibility of Scripture, as truly as against the infallibility of the Church; for no one will say that the Apostles were infallible for nothing, yet we are only morally certain there they were infallible."[30] Notice here that just after categorically stating that the Apostles were simply infallible, he then undermines our full acceptance of this truth by claiming that the Apostles' infallibility is merely "morally certain."

Fourthly, Newman asserted that revelation did not end at the death of the last Apostle. For in *An Essay on the Development of Christian Doctrine* he wrote, "We shall find ourselves unable to fix an historical point at which the *growth of doctrine ceased.* Not on the day of Pentecost, for St. Peter had still to learn at Joppa about the baptism of Cornelius; not at Joppa and Caesarea, for St. Paul had to write his Epistles; *not on the death*

---

29 *Pascendi*, n. 18.
30 *An Essay on the Development of Christian Doctrine* (London, Pickering and co., 1881), p. 81.

*of the last apostle,* for St. Ignatius *had to establish the doctrine of Episcopacy,* not then, nor for many years after, for the canon of the New Testament was still undetermined..."[31] Note, however, that this proposition is condemned in Pius X's Syllabus of Errors: "Revelation, constituting the object of the Catholic faith, was not completed with the Apostles."[32]

On the other hand, many passages of Newman could be cited for his holding the orthodox teaching on this critical teaching of the Church. "Thus, in 1852 he was writing: 'Christian truth is purely of revelation; that revelation we can but explain, we cannot increase, except relatively to our own apprehension.' And in 1858: 'Every Catholic holds that the Christian dogmas were in the Church from the time of the Apostles; that they were ever in their substance what they are now'—i.e., the doctrines existed before the definitions. In *The Idea of a University* Newman wrote: 'What is known in Christianity is just that which is revealed, and nothing more... From the time of the Apostles to the end of the world no strictly new truth can be added to the theological information which the Apostles were inspired to deliver.' And, in accents that echo those of St. Vincent of Lérins and Bossuet: 'The Gospel faith is a definite deposit, a treasure, common to all and the same in every age.' Writing to Acton, Newman defined development as 'a more intimate apprehension, and a more lucid enunciation of the original dogma,' and expressed the view that if St. Clement or St. Polycarp had been asked whether our Lady had been immaculately conceived,

---

31 John Henry Newman, *An Essay on the Development of Christian Doctrine* (London, James Toovey, 1845), p. 107.

32 *Lamentabili Sane,* n. 21 (Dz. 2021).

they would, when the terms of the question had been explained to them, have replied: 'Of course, she was.'"[33]

Fifthly, Newman eluded giving a clear statement about whether the Church ever contradicted herself in teaching the faith. "Is there to be found a clearer case of anticlimax in the substance of its reasoning than in the closing sentence of the third chapter of the *Development of Christian Doctrine*? '.... the one essential question is whether the recognized organ of teaching, the Church herself, acting through Pope or Council as the oracle of heaven, has ever contradicted her own enunciations. If so, the hypothesis which I am advocating is at once shattered; but, till I have positive and distinct evidence of the fact, I am slow to give credence to the existence of so great an improbability.'"[34] Hence "Newman himself has very frequently suffered from selective quotation, without regard to the context and without taking into consideration what he says elsewhere on the subject in question. As Avery Dulles has rightly insisted, 'Newman cannot be studied through excerpts, but only by a grasp of his thinking in its full range.'"[35]

---

33 *Discourses on the Scope and Nature of University Education* (first edition) p. 348; *Tracts Theological and Ecclesiastical* (ed. 1874) p. 287; a letter of February 5, 1871, to Fr. Coleridge, S.J., reproduced in *Letters of J. H. Newman,* edited by Derek Stanford and Muriel Spark (London, 1957); Anthony A. Stephenson, S.J., "The Development and Immutability of Christian Doctrine," *Theological Studies*, vol. 19, n. 4 (December 1, 1958), pp. 531-532.

34 *An Essay on the Development of Christian Doctrine* (London, Basil Montagu Pickering, 1878), p. 121; William Henry Allison, "Was Newman a Modernist?," *The American Journal of Theology*, vol. 14, n. 4, p. 568.

35 Avery Cardinal Dulles, SJ, *Newman* (London and New York, Continuum, 2002), p. 113.

# III
## *Defensive Ambiguity*

Still the primary source of the misunderstanding of Newman comes from Newman himself. For Newman habitually 'economizes' when treating subjects which could cause him to be censured by his superiors:

"Economy" is one of the words of the Newmanian lexicon. The word and thing were, as is known, brought into vogue by the Fathers of the Alexandrine school. A wise economist, instead of at once handing over all his stores for seizure, distributes them piecemeal according to daily requirements. The case of the master is similar, who must proportion his lessons to the actual knowledge of the pupils, keep to himself, hide, "economise" part of the truth. Being for a long time the leader of a religious party, of which the enemy watched for the slightest trip, a conductor of souls fully conscious of the responsibilities of his mission, a teacher by instinct and taste, feeling also an artist's pleasure in the handling of implications and allusions—these, and other causes as well, made Newman, in other respects so loyal, so straightforward, and even sometimes so opinionated, an "economist" of the first order. After all, the question put by the good canon, when at bay, was not so foolish: "What, then, does Dr. Newman mean?"[36] The folly consisted in casting a doubt on the honor of a gentleman, in confusing "economy" with "lying." In truth, almost always, and even in the works which followed his conversion, it is as well to consider whether

---

36 It will be remembered that this is the title of one of Kingsley's pamphlets against Newman.

Newman is not keeping something back, whether the play of adverbs or of adjectives does not cover some reserve or contain some innuendo, whether there is nothing to be read between the lines, whether the printed text, retouched, repolished twenty times, is anything else than a passage of discovery or a temporary expedient. In this delicate art of saying a thing without appearing to say it he is a past-master.[37]

Now was Newman really disguising his thoughts out of fear of being censured? Why else did he anonymously pen his most controversial article in the liberal magazine, *The Rambler*? And this article, *On Consulting the Faithful in Matters of Doctrine*, "was delated to Rome by Bishop Brown of Newport, who denounced it as heretical."[38] Furthermore, he was aware that he was held in suspicion by the Roman authorities of his time.

Wilfrid Ward, his greatest biographer, regards the following five years [after 1859] as the saddest in Newman's life. The Oratorian chafed under the restraint placed upon him. He craved greater freedom to express himself without being pounced upon by the authorities... In 1863 Newman wrote to Miss E. Bowles: 'This age of the Church is peculiar. In former times there was not the extreme centralization now in use. If a private theologian said anything free, another answered him. If the controversy grew, then it went to the bishop. The Holy See was but the court of ultimate appeal. Now if I as a private theologian put anything into print, Propaganda answers me at once. How can I fight with such a chain on my arm? It is like the Persians driven to fight under the lash. There

---

37 Henri Bremont, *The Mystery of Newman* (London, Williams and Norgate, 1907), pp. 5-6.

38 John A. O'Brien, *Giants of the Faith* (New York, Image Books, 1960), p. 172.

was true private judgment in the primitive and medieval schools—there are no schools now, no private judgment (in the religious sense of the phrase), no freedom, that is, of opinion. That is, no exercise of the intellect. No, the system goes on by the tradition of the intellect of former times.'[39]

He was aware that his views were under "a cloud" of suspicion during the long pontificate of Pope Pius IX. In communicating to his friend, Dean Church, the news of his being appointed a cardinal by Pope Leo XIII, Newman wrote: "All the stories which have gone about of my being a half Catholic, a Liberal Catholic, under a cloud, not to be trusted, are now at an end."[40] His famous address, known as the 'Biglietto' speech is his protestation that he had been falsely accused of being a liberal. But it can be argued that Newman opposed a self-defined "liberalism," namely the toleration of small minority denominations in England which he feared would weaken the established Anglican Church. For before his conversion he used the word in this sense. "In June 1830 Newman resigned his membership of the Bible Society because it encouraged 'coming on *common ground* with Dissenters' [i.e. the Evangelicals]: 'I do believe it makes churchmen liberals... it makes them feel a wish to conciliate Dissenters at the expense of truth."[41]

---

39 *Ibid*, p. 173-174.

40 W. Ward, *Life of Cardinal Newman* (1913 ed.), n, 451 f.

41 *The Letters and Diaries of John Henry Newman* (Oxford, Clarendon Press, 1978-2006) vol. 2, pp. 264-5.

# IV
# *A Man is Known by His Friendships*

Could it be that, as Shakespeare said, "methinks thou dost protest too much," when Newman protests that he is not a liberal? Or perhaps Newman was merely branded a liberal in his time for his supporting and associating with certain liberals? For in the *Catholic Enclyclopedia* it is said: "Of Montalembert and Lacordaire he wrote in 1864: 'In their general line of thought and conduct I enthusiastically concur and consider them to be before their age.' ... He was intent on the problems of the time and not alarmed at Darwin's *Origin of Species*."[42] On the other hand, Lacordaire, whom Newman admired, had no qualms about being called a liberal. "It will be recalled that on his deathbed Lacordaire said: 'I die a repentant Christian but an unrepentant Liberal.'"[43] His sympathy for certain Englishmen known to be liberal, however, was more discreet. "In theory Newman, whose co-operation [the English liberal Catholics] naturally desired and to some extent succeeded in obtaining, agreed with this attitude, but its practical application by such writers as Acton and Simpson filled him with misgivings. For Newman throughout his career as a Roman Catholic,[44] however much he regretted the conduct or policy of his ecclesiastical superiors, treated them always with a

---

42 Barry, William, "John Henry Newman," *The Catholic Encyclopedia* (New York, Robert Appleton Company, 1911), vol. 10, p. 798.

43 John A. O'Brian, *op. cit.* (New York, Image Books, 1960), pp. 163-164.

44 And during his career as Anglican too, when he regarded his own bishop as his pope; see *Apologia* (Everyman's ed.), p. 69.

studied deference. It seemed to him that the 'Rambler' writers put forward their views too aggressively and with too much self-confidence, that they treated the episcopate with insufficient respect, and that they were not careful to avoid shocking those of their fellow-churchmen whose faith was old-fashioned. Thus, for instance, in 1861 we find [Lord] Acton writing to [Richard] Simpson, [the two editors of *The Rambler*]:

> I have all the pains in the world to keep Newman in good humor. He is so much riled at what he pleasantly calls your habit of pea-shooting at any dignitary who looks out of the window as you pass along the road, that I am afraid he will not stand by us if we are censured. But he will be very indignant with the authorities, and declares that he agrees with us in principle entirely.[45]

Not only did Newman show friendship and support for certain liberals who lived before and during his lifetime, but after his death he was acclaimed by the very modernists who were condemned by Pius X and who point to Newman as their ideological ancestor.

Newman died before the period of the modernists (about 1890-1910). However, Lawrence Barmann (*Theological Inquiry in an Authoritarian Church: Newman and Modernism*) argues that some of Newman's principles, methods, and conclusions can be construed as analogous to those of the Modernists: for example, the comparison with Loisy's thought on doctrinal development. Loisy and George Tyrrell were condemned in 1907 by the encyclical *Pascendi dominici gregis*. They were not disciples of Newman, nor was Friedrich von Hügel; yet they were influenced

---

45 Gasquet, *Lord Acton and his circle* (London, Burns and Oates, 1906), p. 192; Alec Vidler, *The Modernist Movement in the Catholic Church: Its Origins & Outcome* (Protestant), p. 46.

broadly and deeply by the spirit in which Newman argued, especially by his emphasis upon history and upon human and real experience. An appropriate way to interpret historically the relation of Newman to Modernism is to inquire whether Newman represented an earlier analogue of the later tension between Catholic intellectuals and ecclesiastical authority that led to the condemnation of Modernism. That is, the condemnation of Modernism provided a new historical context for a constructive interpretation of Newman's approach to the tension between theological inquiry and ecclesiastical authority. This interpretation provides insight into Newman's religious outlook and vision for ecclesiology today.[46]

More specifically, Fr. George Tyrrell, who was excommunicated for publicly opposing the encyclical *Pascendi dominici gregis*, which condemned Modernism, claimed that Newman founded the methodology used by the Modernists:

> Listen to what Father Tyrrell, the translator of the *Programme* [*of Modernism*, a reply from some Italian Modernists to *Pascendi*], has said elsewhere: 'The solidarity of Newmanism with Modernism cannot be denied. Newman might have shuddered at his progeny, but it is none the less his. He is the founder of a method which has led to results which he could not have foreseen or desired. The growth of his system has made its divergence from scholasticism clearer every day. If scholasticism is essential to Catholicism, Newman must go overboard and the defiance hurled in the face of history at the Vatican Council and reit-

---

46 Gerard Magill, "The Intellectual Ethos of John Henry Newman," in *Discourse and Context: An Interdisciplinary Study of John Henry Newman* (Carbondale, Southern Illinois University Press, 1993), p. 9.

erated with emphasis by Pius X is superabundantly justified.'[47] Tyrrell does not here call Newman a Modernist; he rather implies that Newman would at least have shrunk from becoming one; but he argues that if Newman had carried through his interpretation of Catholicism consistently, the breach with scholasticism would have been inevitable and Newman would have been forced to break with his logic or place himself among the Modernists. We have seen, however, how Newman shifts his position at the crisis and is inconsistent in his logic."[48]

In December, 1896, we learn that [M. Loisy] was reading Newman [and on December 4 said:] "with enthusiasm." "Je lis toujours Newman avec intérêt." He wrote to Friedrich von Hügel [on December 26]: "Newman must have been the most open-minded theologian that had existed in the Church since Origen."[49]

Father Alfred Loisy, who was also excommunicated for opposing the same encyclical, nevertheless claimed Newman as his guide. "In October 1903, as a result of the furor created over *L'Evangile et l'*église, Loisy published a further explication of his ideas in *Autour d'un petit livre* in which he explicitly claimed Newman as his guide in the theory of development."[50]

---

47 *Hibbert Journal*, January, vol. 6 (1908), p. 243.

48 William Henry Allison, "Was Newman a Modernist?", *The American Journal of Theology*, Vol. 14, n. 4 (Oct. 1910), p. 570-571.

49 *Mémoires pour server a l'histoire religieuse de notre temps*, Vol. I, 421, 426.

50 "S'appliquant à l'histoire des dogmes, il choisit pour guide le Cardinal Newman et reprit son idée du développement chrétien, pour l'opposer aux systèmes de MM. Harnack et A. Sabatier." ["Applied to the history of dogmas, he chooses Cardinal Newman as his guide and resumed his idea of Christian development, to oppose it to the systems of Mr. Harnack and Mr. A. Sabatier."] (Alfred Loisy, *Autour d'un Petit Livre*, 2d edition (Paris: Alphonse Picard et Fils, 1903), p. 7).

Newman served as a mentor to a third leading modernist theologian, Friedrich von Hügel:

Although Newman's influence on both Tyrrell and Loisy is undeniable, even if not completely definable, on von Hügel it was both earlier and more pervasive in his life, and ultimately more lasting. Raised in the Austrian embassies at Florence and then in Brussels, where his father was ambassador, Friedrich von Hügel never experienced the structures and socialization of formal education at any level, having always been tutored privately. At the age of seventeen, while undergoing a religious crisis in his adolescent life, the young baron first read one of Newman's books, *Loss and Gain*, which, he later observed, was the first work to make him "realize the intellectual might and grandeur of the Catholic position."[51] In the immediately ensuing years he read the *Apologia, Anglican Difficulties, Grammar of Assent*, and others of Newman's works, and when he first contacted Newman in 1874, he told him that these books 'at different times and in different ways formed distinct epochs in my young intellectual and religious life. Such intellectual discipline as I have had, I owe it to your books.'[52] At the age of twenty-four, von Hügel spent a week in Birmingham in order to have several interviews with Newman. Significantly, the topics on which von Hügel wanted to pick Newman's brain included human certainty about God, scholastic philosophy, papal infallibility, and the papal temporal

---

51 Friedrich von Hügel to Henry Ignatius Dudley Ryder, August 18, 1890, in Lawrence Barmann, *Baron Friedrich van Hügel and the Modernist Crisis in England* (Cambridge: Cambridge University Press, 1972), p. 5.

52 Friedrich von Hügel to John Henry Newman, December 13, 1874, in Barmann, *Baron Friedrich von Hügel*, pp. 56.

power. When Newman died fourteen years later, von Hügel wrote to Father Ryder and the Oratory Community to express his sympathy and to indicate how much he owed Newman personally, concluding that he talked Newman even oftener than he knew.[53] Newman's influence on individuals who would later be labeled modernist was, clearly, both broad and deep.[54]

More important than the claim by modernists of Newman's ideological parentage is the disfavor of the ecclesiastical authorities toward certain writings of his. Foremostly Newman's theory on the development of Christian doctrine has been often suspected of falling under the condemnation of Rome. "It was disputed at the time at which of the Modernist leaders the Encyclical was mainly aimed. Probably it was primarily directed against Loisy. But in some passages we may find a direct condemnation of the views of Blondel and Laberthonnière; and in others Bergson, or at least his followers in the Roman priesthood, seem to be attacked. Some writers have held that the views of Newman are covertly aimed at. And certainly his teaching of *The Development of Christian Doctrine* is quite irreconcilable with the Papal views."[55] Newman himself refers to Rome's opposition to his theory. "I am told from Rome that I am guilty of the late Definition [of Papal Infallibility] by my work on Development, so orthodox has it been found in principle..."[56]

---

53 Friedrich von Hügel to Henry Ignatius Dudley Ryder, August 18, 1890, in Barmann, *Baron Friedrich van Hügel*, p. 6.

54 Lawrence Barmann, "Theological Inquiry in an Authoritarian Church: Newman and Modernism," in *Discourse and Context: An Interdisciplinary Study of John Henry Newman*, ed. by Gerard Magill (Carbondale, Southern Illinois University Press, 1993), p. 183.

55 Gardner, Percy, *Modernism in the English Church*, 1926.

56 Letter of Cardinal Newman (February 5, 1871) addressed to Father Coleridge, and printed in *The Month* for March 1903.

# V
# *Pervading Spirit of Skepticism*

A common criticism in Rome of Newman's *An Essay on the Development of Doctrine* was that it was imbued with a spirit of skepticism. "He had discovered, perhaps to his surprise, that while the Roman theologians disagreed with his expression of the theory, they objected to the *Essay* above all because it included skeptical language about the capacity of the human reason to attain certainty in matters of faith (especially when those matters of faith were historical)."[57] Anglicans also noted that Newman was skeptical. "[The Anglican bishop of St. David's] Connop Thirlwall judged Newman's mind to be 'essentially skeptical and sophistical' ... [Thomas Henry] Huxley said he could compile a 'Primer of Infidelity' from three of Newman's works."[58]

Newman partly attributed these accusations of skepticism to the influence of the Anglican Bishop Joseph Butler on his own thinking:

> It was at about this date, I suppose, that I read Bishop Butler's *Analogy*; the study of which has been to so many, as it was to me, an era in their religious opinions... if I may attempt to determine what I most gained from it, it lay in two points, which I shall have an opportunity of dwelling on in the sequel; they are the underlying principles of a great portion of my

---

57 Owen Chadwick, *From Bossuet to Newman* (Cambridge, Cambridge University Press, 1987), p. 174.

58 i.e. Tract 85, the *Essay on Ecclesiastical Miracles* of 1843 and the *Essay on Development* (Huxley, *Essays on Controverted Questions* (1892), p. 471).

teaching. First, the very idea of an analogy between the separate works of God leads to the conclusion that the system which is of less importance is economically or sacramentally connected with the more momentous system... Secondly, Butler's doctrine that Probability is the guide of life, led me, at least under the teaching to which a few years later I was introduced, to the question of the logical cogency of Faith, on which I have written so much. Thus to Butler I trace those two principles of my teaching, which have led to a charge against me both of fancifulness and of skepticism.[59]

---

59 Newman, *Apologia Pro Vita* (London, Longmans, Green, and Co., 1908), pp. 113-114.

# VI
# *A Kantian versus Scholastic Philosophical Foundation*

Besides Butler, Newman's writings have a marked influence from the philosophy of Immanuel Kant, who is commonly known to have provided the philosophic groundwork of Modernism,[60] even though Newman categorically twice declares, "'I never read a word of Kant'" in letters to S. W. Lilly in 1884-5,[61] "but he also said, 'I never read a word of Coleridge.'" This latter remark is as Wilfrid Ward says, "not the only instance in which his memory was in later years at fault."[62] "He possessed, it is true, a copy of Meiklejohn's translation of Kant's *Critique of Pure Reason* (1855), and its leaves are cut from the beginning to the doctrine on categories."[63] "Newman must have learned something about Kant from Pusey's book, which he read after its publication in 1828. However, while Pusey has studied Kant rather thoroughly, Newman has got only some vague impressions."[64] "[W. S.] Lilly declares, that 'the philosophical basis of the Oxford Movement was indirectly derived from Kant.' 'Coleridge was,' according to Lilly, 'the first among English thinkers to study and understand Kant,

60 Cf. "The Encyclical of His Holiness Pius X on the Doctrines of the Modernists," edited by Thomas E. Judge, p. 104.

61 *Letters and Diaries of J. H. Newman*, ed. by C. S. Dessain, xxi, p. 391 (*Newman to Lilly*, 4 Aug. 1884); xxxi, p. 7 (*Newman to Lilly*, 7 Jan. 1885).

62 Wilfrid Ward, *The Life of H. Card. Newman* (1912), vol. 1, p. 58 n. 2.

63 Johannes Artz, *Newman in Contact with Kant's Thought* in *The Journal of Theological Studies*, vol. 31 (1980), n. 2, p. 517.

64 Ibid. p. 518.

to assimilate his teaching, and to reproduce it in a new form... I am concerned with his effect upon... the Tractarian Movement. Cardinal Newman, in a paper published in the *British Critic* in 1839, reckons him one of his precursors, as 'providing a philosophical basis for it, as instilling a higher philosophy into inquiring minds than they had hitherto been accustomed to accept.'"[65] "[Coleridge] used to insist, to Kant that he owes, with much else, that distinction between Understanding and Reason—*Verstand* and *Vernunft*—which is one of his fundamental positions; which, indeed, he considered essential to any profitable study of philosophy."[66]

Not only was Newman indebted to Kant, but also to Hegel. For as Msgr. Joseph Clifford Fenton wrote:

It was Newman's contention that the intense theological study which had preceded the *Ineffabilis Deus* [Apostolic Constitution of Pope Pius IX on the Immaculate Conception] "had brought Catholic Schools into union about it, while it secured the accuracy of each." He believed that each of the two schools of thought which had previously existed on the subject of our Lady's Immaculate Conception "had its own extreme points eliminated, and they became one, because the truth to which they converged was one." Newman seemed to assert that the only means of doctrinal progress was along the Hegelian lines of thesis, antithesis, and synthesis. He apparently imagined, that when two groups are opposed on some issue, the ultimate resolution can come only through a sort of compromise, in which the "extreme" points of both opposing theories are abandoned while all the contestants unite in their adherence to a middle position. He seems not to have

---

65 W. S. Lilly, *Ancient Religion and Modern Thought* (London, 1884), p. ii, resp. 59-61.

66 *Ibid*, p. 60

considered the possibility of a situation in which two parties might debate, and one turn out to have defended a truth which the other attacked.[67]

What especially occasioned Newman to carry with him the liberal philosophies which infected the Oxford Movement into the true Church was his lack of a scholastic formation. Moreover, on the person level, the study of philosophy did not appeal to him. "[Newman] is by nature a poet, by necessity rather than choice a metaphysician and historian. Truth finds him through the imagination, is real only as it comes to him in image and breathing form, a being instinct with life. And so he hates the abstract and loves the concrete; a truth grows real to him only when it is so embodied as to speak to the imagination and fill it."[68] He even distrusted abstract, deductive reasons. Instead his reasoning was more existential and empirical. "I had a great dislike of paper logic. For myself, it was not logic that carried me on; as well might one say that the quicksilver in the barometer changes the weather. It is the concrete being that reasons; pass a number of years, and I find my mind in a new place; how? the whole man moves; paper logic is but the record of it."[69]

---

67 *John Henry Newman and the Vatican Definition of Papal Infallibility*, in *The American Ecclesiastical Review*, vol. 113, n. 4 (Oct., 1945), p. 313.

68 A. M. Fairbairn, "Catholicism and Religious Thought," *The Contemporary Review,* vol. 47 (May 1885), pp. 663-664.

69 Newman, *Apologia Pro Vita* (London, Longmans, Green, and Co., 1908), p. 169.

# VII
## *"No Salvation Outside the Church"*

How then can one analyze such writings if Newman is elusive on essential points and lacks a solid philosophical basis needed to express oneself with clarity? Let us turn to some great Catholic minds who have spoken about Newman. They certainly praise his eloquence and intellectual insights into understanding human nature. But for a thing to be good, it must be entirely good. Hence, let us see where they find fault with Newman's writings. And so, instead of trusting our own analysis, let us turn to a renown theologian, Msgr. Joseph Clifford Fenton, firstly for his surmise of Cardinal Newman's view of the dogma, *Extra ecclesiam, nulla salus.*

The teaching that the dogma of the necessity of the Church for salvation admits of exceptions is, in the last analysis, a denial of the dogma as it has been stated in the authoritative declarations of the ecclesiastical magisterium and even as it is expressed in the axiom or formula *Extra ecclesiam nulla salus.* It is important to note that such teaching is found in Cardinal Newman's last published study on this subject, a study incorporated into his *Letter to the Duke of Norfolk,* perhaps the least valuable of all his published works. Because of Newman's great influence in the field of contemporary theological studies, it will be helpful to see how he treated this subject in the *Letter.*

[The Old Catholic and apostate Arnold Harris] Matthew, who held ultimately that Catholics were simply not bound to hold anything like the teaching that no one can be saved outside the Catholic Church, was enthusiastic in his praise of Newman's explanation. He claimed that the Cardinal had "dealt with the question in such a masterly way that it is impossible to improve upon what he says."[70] As a group, the theologians of the Catholic Church have shown no disposition whatsoever to share Matthew's enthusiasm for this section of Newman's teaching.

In his *Letter to the Duke of Norfolk*, Newman dealt with the Church's necessity for salvation, not for its own sake, but only as a teaching that he considered as offering "the opportunity of a legitimate minimizing."[71] Despite the fact that he complained when his theological opponents designated him as a minimizer, he set out to show that the dogmas taught in the Vatican Council's constitution *Pastor aeternus* were subject to legitimate minimizing.[72] He tried to support his contention by appealing to the example of the dogma that there is no salvation outside the Catholic Church. Hence it was from this angle that he approached the teaching on the necessity of the Church for salvation.

Newman taught that the principle "out of the Church, and out of the faith, is no salvation" admits of exceptions. He believed that what Pope Pius IX had taught in his encyclical *Quanto conficiamur moerore* indicated the existence of such exceptions.[73] In

---

70 Matthew, in his chapter, *Extra Ecclesiam Salus Nulla*, in the symposium, *Ecclesia: The Church of Christ*, edited by Arnold Harris Matthew (London, Burns and Oats, 1906), p. 148.

71 In *Certain Difficulties Felt by Anglicans in Catholic Teaching* (London: Longmans, Green, and Co., 1896), II, 334.

72 Msgr. Joseph Clifford Fenton, *John Henry Newman and the Vatican Definition of Papal Infallibility*, in *The American Ecclesiastical Review*, vol. 113, n. 4 (Oct., 1945), 300-20.

73 In *Certain Difficulties Felt by Anglicans in Catholic Teaching* (London: Longmans, Green, and Co., 1896), II, p. 335 ff.

support of his contention, he quotes the following lines from the encyclical:

*We and you know*, that those who lie under invincible ignorance as regards our most holy religion, and who, diligently observing the natural law and its precepts, which are engraven by God on the hearts of all, and prepared to obey God, lead a good and upright life, are able, by the operation of the power of divine light and grace, to obtain eternal life.[74]

According to the *Letter to the Duke of Norfolk*, these words of Pope Pius IX conveyed what Newman called "the doctrine of invincible ignorance—or, that it is possible to belong to the soul of the Church without belonging to the body." He concluded his treatment of the dogma with this question: "Who would at first sight gather from the wording of so forcible a universal ['Out of the Church, and out of the faith, is no salvation'], that an exception to its operation, such as this, so distinct, and, for all we know, so very wide, was consistent with holding it?"[75]

If Newman's words mean anything, they assert that the Church holds and proposes as "a dogma, which no Catholic can ever think of disputing," a statement which it contradicts at the very same time. He claims that the doctrine "Out of the Church, and out of the faith, is no salvation" is a dogma of the Church, a truth revealed by God to be held on divine faith by all men. This dogma is set forth as a universal negative proposition, something which is contradicted by a particular affirmative. And Newman taught here that the particular affirmative proposition contradicting this very universal negative dogma is true. He believed that in at least one definite case, which may

---

74 *Ibid*, p. 335 ff.
75 *Ibid.*, 336.

have a very wide application, there can be salvation outside the faith and outside the Church.

Newman believed that it was "consistent" to hold at the same time that there is no salvation outside the Church and outside the faith. Obviously, there could be no more effective way of reducing the teaching on the necessity of the Church for the attainment of eternal salvation to an empty formula than the explanation advanced by Newman in what are probably the least felicitous pages of all his published works. That explanation is certainly one of those reproved in the encyclical letter *Humani generis*.

Some Catholic authors attempted to explain the dogma of the Church's necessity for the attainment of salvation by saying that the Church is only the ordinary means, and that it is still possible, in extraordinary cases, for a man to attain the Beatific Vision outside the Church. At the same time, they resolutely claimed, as Newman had done, that it is a Catholic dogma that there is no salvation outside the Church. Manifestly, according to this explanation, the dogma would be nothing more than a vain formula, something which the very people who accept it as a dogma would be expected to treat, for all practical purposes, as untrue."[76]

---

76 Msgr. Joseph Clifford Fenton, *The Catholic Church and Salvation: In the Light of Recent Pronouncements of the Holy See* (Westminster (MA), The Newman Press, 1958), pp. 124-126.

# VIII
## *Minimalism*

In applying this defined dogma of there being no salvation outside of the Church, Newman while accepting
the teaching in principle nevertheless undermines it in
practice through minimalism. Firstly, hear Newman's
optimism about the salvation of the Anglicans whom he
left behind when he entered the Catholic Church:

> As to the prospect of those countless multitudes of
> a country like this, who apparently have no super-
> natural vision of the next world at all, and die without
> fear because they die without thought, with these,
> alas! I am not here concerned. But the remarks I have
> been making suggest *much of comfort*, when we look
> out into what is called the *religious world in all its va-
> rieties*, whether it be the High Church section, or the
> Evangelical, whether it be in the Establishment, or in
> Methodism, or in Dissent, so far as there seems to be
> real earnestness and invincible prejudice. One cannot
> but hope that that written Word of God, for which
> they desire to be jealous, though exhibited to them in
> a mutilated form and in a translation unsanctioned
> by Holy Church, is of incalculable blessing to their
> souls, and may be, through God's grace, the divine
> instrument of bringing *many to contrition and to a
> happy death who have received no sacrament since
> they were baptized in their infancy*. One cannot hope
> but that the Anglican Prayer Book, with its Psalter
> and Catholic prayers, even though these, in the trans-
> lation, have passed through heretical intellects, may
> retain so much of its old virtue as to cooperate with
> divine grace in the instruction and *salvation of a*

*large remnant.* In these and many other ways, even in England, and much more in Greece, the difficulty is softened which is presented to the imagination by the view of such large populations, who, though called Christian, are not Catholic or orthodox in creed.[77]

However, the 1864 Syllabus of Errors of Pope Pius IX condemns such optimism by its condemnation of the following proposition: "Good hope at least is to be entertained of the eternal salvation of all those who are not at all in the true Church of Christ."[78]

But it was not only in his *Letter to the Duke of Norfolk* that Newman expressed his belief that certain non-Catholics may belong to the soul, but not the visible body of the Church, and hence ought to be unquieted about their lack of membership in the Church and need not be converted. "On the very day of his reception into the Catholic Church, he wrote to his sister Jemima that his acceptance of the claims of the Roman Catholic Church was entirely 'consistent with believing, as I firmly do, that individuals in the English Church are invisibly knit into that True Body of which they are not outwardly members—and consistent too with thinking it highly injudicious, indiscreet, wanton to interfere with them in particular cases.'"[79] His optimism is based on his "firm belief that grace was to be found within

---

77 Newman, *Certain Difficulties Felt by Anglicans in Catholic Teaching: In Twelve Lectures addressed in 1850 to the Party of the Religious Movement of 1833,* (London, Longmans, Green, and Co., 1901), vol. 2, pp. 356-357.

78 Encyclical *Quanto conficiamur,* Aug. 10, 1863, etc. (*Syllabus of Errors,* n. 17).

79 Newman to Jemima Mozley, October 9, 1845, *The Letters and Diaries of John Henry Newman* (London, Oxford University Press, Nelson and Sons Ltd, 1961), vol. 11, p.14.

the Anglican Church."[80] He even argued that "it does not follow, because there is no Church but one, which has the Evangelical gifts and privileges to bestow, that therefore no one can be saved without the intervention of that one Church..."[81]

Consequently, the conversion of England to the faith would not be as important to Newman as it was to England's Recusant Catholics, who risked life and limb to keep the faith during times of Anglican persecutions. For in his journal for January 21, 1863, he wrote: "At Propaganda, conversions, and nothing else, are the proof of doing anything. Everywhere with Catholics, to make converts is doing something; and not to make them, is 'doing nothing.'... But I am altogether different... I am afraid to make hasty converts of educated men, lest they should not have counted the cost, and should have difficulties after they have entered the Church... [T]he Church must be prepared for converts, as well as converts prepared for the Church."[82] Newman was a minimalist to the end.

---

80 Newman, *Apologia Pro Vita* (London, Longmans, Green, and Co., 1908), p. 227.

81 *Certain Difficulties Felt by Anglicans in Catholic Teaching* (London, Longmans, Green and Co., 1900), vol. 2, p. 335.

82 John Henry Newman, *Autobiographical Writings*, ed. Henry Tristram (London, Sheed & Ward, 1956), 257-258.

# IX
## *Papal Infallibility*

Msgr. Fenton also finds fault with Newman's treatment of papal infallibility. Hence he laments, "As a result his attitude towards the Vatican Council's definition of papal infallibility has been put on a level with the rest of his teachings. The effect has been most unfortunate. Some Catholics, and not a few of those outside the true Church, have been led to accept on the authority of Newman what, in the last analysis, is an imperfect and inexact statement on the conciliar doctrine."[83] Newman seems to have held that the pope could not have taught infallibly before the dogma was defined. For as he wrote, the pope "could not fulfil the conditions of an *ex cathedra* utterance, if he did not actually mean to fulfil them . . . and who will dream of saying . . . that Honorius in the 7th century did actually intend to exert that infallible teaching voice which has been dogmatically recognized in the nineteenth?"[84]

Msgr. Fenton notes that for Newman papal infallibility is only a theological opinion:

Yet by all means the most important feature of Newman's view of papal infallibility was his absolute insistence that this doctrine should be treated as a matter of mere theological opinion. A detailed statement of Newman's thought on the quality of

---

83 Msgr. Joseph Clifford Fenton, "John Henry Newman and the Vatican Definition of Papal Infallibility," *The American Ecclesiastical Review*, vol. 113, n. 4 (October 1945), p. 300.

84 John Henry Newman, *A Letter Addressed to His Grace the Duke of Norfolk on Occasion of Mr. Gladstone's Recent Expostulation* (London: Pickering, 1875), p. 108.

assent due to this thesis is found in a letter to Dr. Edward Bouverie Pusey.

> Applying this principle [that is, that a man may be obliged to believe a doctrine on grounds either of faith or 'religiousness'] to the Pope's Infallibility, (N.B. this of course is mine own opinion only, *meo periculo*) a man will find it a religious duty to *believe* it or may safely *disbelieve* it, in *proportion* as he thinks it probable or improbable that the Church might or will define it, or does hold it, and that it is the doctrine of the Apostles. For myself, (still to illustrate what I mean, not as arguing) I think that the Church *may* define it (i.e. it possibly may turn out to belong to the original *depositum*), but that she will not ever define it; and again I do not see that she can be said to hold it. She never can simply *act* upon it, (being undefined as it is) and I believe never has—moreover, on the other hand, I think that there is a good deal of evidence, on the very surface of history and the Fathers in its favor. On the whole then I hold it; but I should account it no sin if, on the grounds of reason, I doubted it.[85]

He could look with equanimity on statements contradicting his own tenets on the subject of the Holy Father's infallibility as long as these statements were presented as opinions which could be accepted or rejected freely. He is intolerant and indignant when such teachings are offered as dogmatic truth.

> Let me observe then that in former years, *and now*, I have considered the theological differences between us as unimportant in themselves; that is, such as to be simply compatible with a reception

85 Wilfrid Ward, *The Life of John Henry Cardinal Newman* (London, Longmans, Green and Co., 1912), II, 221. The letter was written March 23, 1867.

both by you and by me on the whole theological teaching of the Church in the widest sense of the word teaching; and again now, and in former years, too, I have considered one phenomenon in you to be 'momentous,' nay, portentous, that you will persist in calling the said unimportant, allowable, inevitable differences, which must occur between mind and mind, not unimportant, but of great moment. In this utterly uncatholic, not so much opinion as feeling and sentiment, you have grown in the course of years, whereas I consider that I remain myself in the same temper of forbearance and sobriety which I have ever wished to cultivate.

His charge against [William G.] Ward is that "you are doing your best to make a party in the Catholic Church, and in St. Paul's words are dividing Christ by exalting your opinions into dogmas." The letter ends on that note of harshness which Newman seemed to reserve for those who differed from him on the question of papal infallibility.

I protest then again, not against your tenets, but against what I must call your schismatic spirit. I disown your intended praise of me, viz. that I hold your theological opinions in "the greatest aversion," and I pray God that I may never denounce, as you do, what the Church has not denounced.[86]

Newman's own attitude towards the theological details of the doctrine of papal infallibility is quite clearly expressed in a letter to Mr. Henry Wilberforce, written July 21, 1867. In this letter he reveals himself as not greatly concerned about the extent and the subject of ecclesiastical inerrancy. The only matter of moment to him is the fact that the Church itself is infallible. He holds himself bound to accept on divine

---

86 Ward, *op. cit.*, p. 232 f.

faith only what is universally taught and universally believed. He acknowledges that the arguments set forth in favor of papal infallibility are not such as to convince him that this doctrine falls into the class of those truths which have been expounded and accepted always and everywhere within the Church. It is Newman's contention that, should the doctrine of papal infallibility really belong to the divine message, the purity of his own faith is saved by the fact that he believes it implicitly in accepting as the revealed word of God everything thus presented by the Catholic Church. Thus Newman's stand did not involve any denial on his part that the doctrine of papal infallibility is actually a part of divine public revelation. He was perfectly willing to admit that this teaching was probably included in God's message to mankind. His whole polemic was directed towards withholding from the doctrine of papal infallibility anything more than an implicit assent of divine faith. Explicitly he would concede it only the status of an opinion.

The pertinent passage, although somewhat long, is far too important to be neglected by one who seeks to understand Newman's attitude towards the Vatican definition.

For myself I have never taken any great interest in the question of the limits and seat of infallibility. I was converted simply because the Church was to last to the end, and that no communion answered to the Church of the first ages but the Roman Communion, both in substantial likeness and in actual descent. And so to faith, my great principle was: *Securus judicat orbis terrarium*.[87] So I say now and in

---

87 I. e., in Newman's own translation, "The universal Church, in her judgments, is sure of the Truth" (Saint Augustine, *Contra Epistolam Parmeniani*, bk. 3, c. 3, n. 23 (PL 43, 101)).

all these questions of detail I say to myself, I believe whatever the Church teaches as the voice of God—and this or that particular inclusively, if she teaches this—it is this *fides implicita* which is our comfort in these irritating times. And I cannot go beyond this—I see arguments here, arguments there—I incline one way today another tomorrow on the whole I more than incline in one direction but I do not dogmatize—and I detest any dogmatism where the Church has not clearly spoken. And if I am told: 'The Church has spoken,' then I ask when? and if, instead of having anything plain shown me, I am put off with a string of arguments, or some strong words of the Pope himself, I consider this a sophistical evasion, I have only an opinion at best (not faith) that the Pope is infallible, and a string of arguments can only end in an opinion—and I comfort myself with the principle: *Lex dubia non obligat*—what is not taught universally, what is not believed universally, has no claim on me—and, if it be true after all and divine, my faith in it is included in the *implicita fides* which I have in the Church.[88]

Msgr. Fenton then gives Newman's view of papal infallibility after it had been defined:

Newman's original position in the infallibility controversy had been in favor of treating this doctrine as an opinion. It was basically on this point that he lashed out against his opponents before the Council, and it was with this in view that he deplored the attempts at definition within the Council and for a time refused to acknowledge the *de fide* status of the teaching even after the Council had spoken. Finally after there could be no doubt concerning the judgment of the great body of faithful, he found a means of rees-

---

88 Ward *op. cit.*, pp. 234 ff.; Fenton, *op. cit.*, pp. 301-305.

tablishing the domain of opinion in this field. The instrument that he employed was his beloved doctrine of 'minimizing.' Newman asserted that the Church "has ever shown the utmost care to contract, as far as possible, the range of truths and the sense of propositions, of which she demands this absolute reception [of the divine faith]."[89] As for the Church's own pronouncements, according to Newman's theory, "She speaks only when it is necessary to speak; but hardly has she spoken out magisterially some great general principle, when she sets her theologians to work to explain her meaning in the concrete, by strict interpretation of its wording, by the illustration of its circumstances, and by the recognition of exceptions, in order to make it as tolerable as possible, and the least of a temptation to self-willed, independent, or wrongly educated minds."[90]

The dogmatic pronouncements with which minimizing is concerned fall into two classes. Some are positive statements of doctrine. Others are negative in form, presented as condemnations of teaching judged inacceptable by the Church. For all practical purposes, the meaning of any proposition in either class must be determined by theologians, which decisions may be accurate, but are certainly never binding.

The negative judgments of the Church, qualifying some proposition as heretical, erroneous, or the like, are primarily commands issued to Catholics to avoid these propositions in teaching. The judgment about the meaning of the condemned doctrine belongs to the theologian, and hence, according to Newman's minimism, to the domain of opinion. The affirmative propositions, on the other hand, with the exception

---

89 *Difficulties of Anglicans,* II, *op.cit.,* p.320.
90 *Ibid,* p. 321.

of those dealing directly with the Godhead or with our Lady and the Saints "are but general, and so far, in consequence, admit of exceptions in their actual application these exceptions being determined either by other authoritative utterances, or by the scrutinizing vigilance, acuteness, and subtlety of the *Schola Theologorum*."[91]

Such was the doctrine set forth by Newman in the famed *Letter to the Duke of Norfolk*. Unfortunately, the rancor which he had always felt towards the leaders in the movement for the definition manifests itself in the *Letter* in such a way as to make it very tiresome reading. Newman never loses an opportunity for an expression of bitterness towards a group which included, after all, the leading Prelates of Christendom. He has only expressions of courtesy for the bumbling politician who had ventured to attack the Church of God. He has only expressions of sympathy for those opponents of the definition who had left the Church. His harsh words are reserved for a group that included men like Archbishops Spalding and Manning. In 1872 he had not a word to retract from the violent letter he had sent to Bishop Ullathorne.[92] In the *Letter to the Duke of Norfolk* he withdraws this lamentable document only to the extent of asserting that it had not been meant for the public eye.[93] Indeed, the *Letter to the Duke of Norfolk* seems to have been considered by Newman himself as an attack on Archbishop Manning as much as a defense of the Catholic body against the libels of Gladstone.[94] It is characteristic of the rela-

---

91 *Ibid*, p. 334.
92 Cf. Wilfrid Ward, *op. cit.*, p. 559.
93 *Difficulties of Anglicans*, II, *op. cit.*, p. 301.
94 Cf. Wilfrid Ward, *op. cit.*, p. 402.

tions of the two great English churchmen that, when the then Cardinal Prefect of Propaganda, Cardinal Franchi, wrote to Archbishop Manning on the subject of censurable propositions in the *Letter to the Duke of Norfolk*, Manning hastened to reply begging that no public action be taken against Fr. Newman, and giving as his first and principal reason the assertion that "The heart of the revered Fr. Newman is as right and as Catholic as it is possible to be."[95]

As a whole, Newman's stand on the doctrine of papal infallibility was doctrinally inexact and unfortunate in its influence. In his controversial efforts against the definition, he seems never to have adverted to the factor which rendered this conciliar act, not only beneficial, but morally necessary to the Church of God. The great ecclesiologists of the Golden Age, almost without exception, had insisted upon the infallibility of the Holy Father's definitive dogmatic pronouncements. They had pointed to the fact that his decisions were irreformable of themselves, whether he spoke in concert with the rest of the apostolic college, or alone in his capacity as the supreme teacher of the true Church of Jesus Christ. The long list of theologians cited by the Louvain faculty in its petition to the Vatican Council covers only a portion of the body of classical ecclesiologists who taught this doctrine. Men like St. Robert [Bellarmine], Francis Suarez, Francis Sylvius, and John Wiggers considered this teaching as a part of the deposit of Catholic faith.

The infamous Gallican Articles darkened the theology of the eighteenth and the early nineteenth centuries. The Gallicans did not simply deny papal in-

_____

95 Dom Cuthbert Butler, *The Life and Times of Bishop Ullathorne* (New York, Benziger Brothers, 1926), II. p. 101.

fallibility, but they would recognize as infallible only those pronouncements which the Holy Father makes in concert with the Catholic bishops throughout the world. The confusion caused by this politico-theological doctrine manifested itself in a relatively poor quality of teaching *De Romano Pontifice* in mid-nineteenth century theology. Only an occasional ecclesiologist like Patrick Murray of Maynooth managed to achieve the clarity and adequacy which had been characteristic of this tract in former years.[96] As a result of the Gallican teachings there had been a regress rather than a progress in an important portion of theology. The definition of papal infallibility was meant to remove this harm from the Church. Unfortunately, Newman seemed unaware of the immediate issue and of its chief implications.

Acton, who was in constant touch with Newman during the time of the infallibility debates and who was sympathetic to Newman's attitude, seems to have considered the great Oratorian's explanation of the Vatican decrees as being, for all intents and purposes, an emptying of their content. Writing to "dear Mr. Gladstone" in December 1874, Acton made no secret of the fact that it was his wish "to make the evils of Ultramontanism so manifest that men will shrink from them, and so explain away or stultify the Vatican Council as to make it innocuous."[97] After the *Letter to the Duke of Norfolk* had appeared, Acton, apparently still unwilling to do other than "explain

---

96 Murray, the outstanding ecclesiologist of the nineteenth century, is among those accused by Newman of attempting "to bring in a new theory of Papal Infallibility." (Cf. Ward, *op. cit.*, II, pp.152 ff.).

97 *Selections from the Correspondence of the First Lord Acton* (London: Longmans, Green and Co., 1917), I, p. 147.

away" the Vatican definitions, announced to Lady Blennerhassett that "Newman's conditions would make it possible, technically, to accept the whole of the decrees."[98] Even before the Council had made its definition Newman had written to Mr. O'Neill Daunt, contending that "if anything is passed, it will be in so mild a form, as practically to mean little or nothing."[99]

The most unfortunate effect of this attitude on the part of Newman has been the emergence of an opinion that, after all the Vatican definition of papal infallibility was of little import. This impression has been spread, not so much by Newman's own writings, which of themselves are not very convincing on this point, as by Wilfrid Ward's official biography of Newman. Ward's *Life*, one of the few really influential modern Catholic works in the English language, sees the issues only through the eyes of Newman himself. Newman's opponents are, for Wilfrid Ward, only the "untheological school,"[100] and the persons who have the temerity to question Newman's position are "good but not far-seeing people,"[101] or "men whose education was not equal to their piety."[102] Without the faintest attempt to appeal to evidence, he leads his readers to believe that the Vatican Council saw a conflict between two groups of extremists, his own father and M. Louis Veuillot on one side against men like Dollinger on the other. The actual definition is supposed to have represented a victory for certain moderates, among whom Newman himself was to be found. Something of the same spirit has gone into the writing of

---

98 *Ibid.*, p. 155.
99 Ward, *op. cit.*, I, p. 299.
100 Cf. *ibid.*, p. 282.
101 Cf. *ibid.*, p. 279.
102 Cf. *ibid,*, p. 280.

Dom Cuthbert Butler's *The Vatican Council*. It is principally from this last-named book that Dr. Trevor Gervase Jalland has taken what he regards as the modern Catholic attitude towards papal infallibility, the impression that this doctrine means very little in the dogma of the Catholic Church. It is regrettable that Dr. Jalland can give to the non-Catholic scholarly world such an ill-advised description of Catholic attitude towards the definition as that which he has taken from Butler: "Rather does it seem to give point to Salmon's gibe—or was it Whateley's?—that the Pope is infallible so long as he defines nothing."[103]

Actually, the opinion of Newman on the definition of papal infallibility is only a kind of unwarranted exception to the theological explanation of the decrees. In the light of the traditional and scientific exposition of papal infallibility, found at its best in works like Billot's *De Ecclesia*, Newman's position is inexact and his uncritical apologists are misleading.

Some popular accounts of Newman's life seem calculated to make us believe that his position on the Vatican Council's definition was basically quite satisfactory. Such a belief would be inaccurate, and harmful both to the Church and to Newman himself. The divine message which we possess within the Catholic Church is too precious a thing to be obscured by the unfortunate theory of even as great a man as Newman. Furthermore, his capacity for good is too powerful to allow us to dally with the notion that his

---

103 *The Vatican Council* (London: Longmans, Green and Co., 1936), II, 228. The sentence is quoted in Jalland's *The Church and the Papacy* (London, Society for Promoting Christian Knowledge, 1944), p. 534.

stand on the infallibility controversies is as valuable as his other contributions to Catholic thought.[104]

Cardinal Newman finally accepted Vatican I's definition of papal infallibility as an article of the faith, but the grounds he had for accepting it was a laicism later adopted at Vatican II. Let us continue to read the analysis of Msgr. Fenton on how Newman submitted to this definition.

As far as he was concerned, even after July 18, 1870, the doctrine of papal infallibility remained an opinion in the last analysis, even though he was quite cheerfully ready to acknowledge that it was highly probable opinion.

Later he was willing to accord it the status of a dogma, but only under conditions which could be made to justify his previous stand. Had he not expressed himself as not too greatly concerned with questions about the seat and the limits of infallibility? Was not his own favorite and ultimate organ of infallibility the consent of the universal Church, the factor described in the phrase *Securus judicat orbis terrarium*, the expression so intimately connected with his own entrance into the true Church? Well, this could be the effective agent for constituting the doctrine of papal infallibility as a Catholic dogma.[105]

After all there was no other way of accepting the definition as a dogma consistent with his principles. It would be absurd to take the Pope's word as a *de fide* profession of his own infallibility. According to Newman the Roman Pontiff's infallibility had hitherto been a matter of opinion, and one who is only

104 Msgr. Joseph Clifford Fenton, *John Henry Newman and the Vatican Definition of Papal Infallibility*, in *The American Ecclesiastical Review*, vol. 113, n. 4 (Oct., 1945), pp. 316-320.

105 *Difficulties of Anglicans*, II, *op. cit.*, p. 372.

probably infallible can certainly not issue a definitive doctrinal judgment on his own authority. The Council was a broken reed, since, apart from any other consideration, it had never been formally closed. Only the *Securus judicat orbem terrarum* is left, and "This indeed is a broad principle by which all acts of the rulers of the Church are ratified." In this passage of my private letter," Newman later explained, "I meant by 'ratified' brought home to us as authentic. At this very moment it is certainly the handy, obvious, and serviceable argument for our accepting the Vatican definition of the Pope's Infallibility."[106]

---

106 *Loc. cit.;* Msgr. Joseph Clifford Fenton, *John Henry Newman and the Vatican Definition of Papal Infallibility*, in *The American Ecclesiastical Review*, vol. 113, n. 4 (Oct., 1945), pp. 315-316.

# X
## *The Church Teaching Replaced by the Church Learning*

But according to Newman, the laity require the assistance of theologians to know what has been infallibly defined. Msgr. Fenton elsewhere explains:

Unfortunately the tendency to misinterpret the function of the private theologian in the Church's doctrinal work is not something new in the English Catholic literature. Cardinal Newman in his *Letter to the Duke of Norfolk* (certainly the least valuable of his published works), supports the bizarre thesis that the final determination of what is really condemned in an authentic ecclesiastical pronouncement is the work of private theologians, rather than of the particular organ of the *ecclesia docens* which has actually formulated the condemnation. The faithful could, according to his theory, find what a pontifical document actually means, not from the content of the document itself, but from the speculations of the theologians.[107]

Note here that Newman considered himself as part of the Church learning. For "when Newman wrote to his bishop concerning the Council's definition of the pope's infallibility, he (in spite of his priestly orders) included himself among the faithful: 'What have *we* done to be treated, as the *faithful* never were treated before?'[108] [Whereas] the regnant theology after Vatican I, such as that of Johann Baptist Franzelin (1816-86), argued that

---

107 *The Doctrinal Authority of Papal Encyclicals*, part 2, Msgr. Joseph Clifford Fenton, *American Ecclesiastical Review*, vol. 121 (September, 1949), p. 219.

108 *Letters and Diaries*, vol. 25, pp. 18-19, emphasis added.

the laity brought nothing to the infallible magisterium except their belief in what was taught."[109] Yet this does not mean that the universal belief of the faithful ought not to be taken into consideration by the Church as an indication of a truth being part of the deposit of the faith. For the belief of the faithful was used as one of the proofs sought when preparing the definition of the Immaculate Conception. The following quotation is from two modern liberal historians, who accept Newman's laicism, yet is still informative:

One of the occasions in the nineteenth century when the *sensus fidelium* was invoked was in the definition of Mary's Immaculate Conception by Pius IX in 1854. In his instruction to the bishops of the Church before issuing a definition, Pius asked them to report back to him on the belief and practices of the faithful in regard to Mary's freedom from sin. The low point [sic]of the *sensus fidelium* in the nineteenth century was, perhaps, the interpretation given to the phrase by the Roman theologian, Cardinal J. B. Franzelin, who interpreted it in terms of what he called "passive infallibility." Whereas the pope and bishops exercised infallibility in an active way by formally teaching the truth to the faithful, the faithful indeed exercised the infallibility of the Church by listening to their leaders and obeying them. This insight led to the formulation of the Church as *ecclesia docens* ('the teaching church'), i.e. the pope and bishops, and the *ecclesia discens* ('the learning church'), i.e. the faithful or the remainder of the Church. Franzelin's narrowing of the understanding of the *infallibilitas in credendo* ["infallibility in believing"] by the faithful eventually became the common opinion of theologians

---

109 Benjamin King, *The Oxford Handbook of John Henry Newman* (Oxford, Oxford University Press, 2018), p. 266.

and would manifest itself in the minority opposition to a more positive understanding [*sic*] of the *sensus fidelium* at Vatican II.[110]

Now to understand the correct role of the laity as being the Church believing and not the Church teaching, let us seek guidance from the theologian who has best clarified the role in the Church in relation to the Church's infallibility. This was the above-mentioned Cardinal Johann Baptist Franzelin, a *peritus*, or consultor, at the First Vatican Council, who was made a Cardinal by Pope Pius IX. He was an expert in Hebrew and a lecturer in Chaldean and Syriac. His lectures and theological writings were highly esteemed in his day.

Firstly, to rightly distinguish the roles of the Church teaching and the Church learning, he cites Saint Augustine affirming that the faithful need to be taught by the hierarchy when expounding the passage: "And you have no need that any man teach you..." (I Jn. 2, 27) as follows: "Then to what purpose is it that we, my brethren, teach you?... to John himself I say... To what purpose have you written an epistle like this? What teaching did you give them? What instruction? What edification?... The teachings of the master from without are a sort of aids and admonitions. He that teaches the hearts, has His chair in heaven."[111]

Franzelin then refutes the objection that since the hierarchy at certain times has poorly defended the faith, while at that same time the faithful better kept the faith, then the hierarchy is superfluous for its preservation as follows:

---

110 John J. Burkhard, *The Routledge Companion to Christian Church* (London, Routledge, 2008), p. 562.

111 St. Augustine, *Homilies on the First Epistle of John*, tract 3, n. 13 cited in footnote 1, Johannes Baptist Franzelin, *Tractatus de divina traditione et scriptura* (Rome, Marietti, 1870), p. 98.

The famous saying of Hilary: "There is more holiness in the ears of the people than in the hearts of the priests,"[112] has only the holiest and most desired meaning, namely that from the communion and agreement of the people with the priests remaining in the unity and consent of the Church is preferred to the teaching of priests who have lapsed from the unity and common faith; it would be very absurd, however, if the *hearts of the priests* were taken limitlessly, or the people were constituted judges of the priests. For in completely reversed order the *hearts of the priests*, meaning the joint knowledge of the faith and the Catholic understanding of the pastors remaining in the unity of the Church, are the ministerial (extrinsic) cause and instrument by which the Spirit of truth forms the *holy ears of the people*, namely their Catholic sense and understanding, of those to whom it belongs to hear, to learn, and to render "obedience to the faith."[113] It can indeed happen that even many bishops of even whole regions defect from the faith, and yet the greater part of the flock of the faithful being constant in the orthodox profession hold forth communion and agreement with the center of unity, i.e. with the See of Peter; yet it cannot happen, that the whole episcopacy could defect, and that this would not remain, by the assistance of the Holy Ghost, the organ of preserving traditions, by which as through the ordinary external magisterium the Spirit would likewise keep and preserve the communion and faith of the Catholic people. Now for this to be true it is not necessarily always required that the whole episcopacy defend and guard with ardor and zeal the orthodox profession against the adversaries; but its constancy

---

112 *Liber contra Arianos vel Auxentium*, n. 6 (PL 10, 613B).
113 Rom. 1, 5.

in the once handed down doctrine suffices, whereby that very constancy remains the immediate, living directing norm and the immediate bond of union for the Catholic people. This can be supported by an event of ecclesiastical history, namely from the history of the strengthening Arianism of the fourth century; but not that which the anonymous author of the dissertation [i.e., Cardinal Newman], "On Consulting the Faithful in Matters of Doctrine" thought could be deduced from this history: "the *Ecclesia docens* is not at every time the active instrument of the Church's infallibility."[114] On the contrary, the exiles of so many Catholic bishops; their constancy against the Arians; the fleeing of the faithful people from the intruded bishops and their communion with the exiled bishops; the account of Sozomen of the greater perseverance of the people in the cities whose bishops were stronger and more constant in the faith;[115] the Antiochian people's threatening to expose the deceits of the Arian

---

114 In the literary magazine, *The Rambler*, July 1859, pp. 218 ff.

115 "Arianism met with similar opposition at the same period in Osröene; but in the Cappadocias, Providence allotted such a divine and most educated pair of men — Basil, the bishop of Cæsarea in that country, and Gregory, bishop of Nazianzen. Syria and the neighboring provinces, and more especially the city of Antioch, were plunged into confusion and disorder; for the Arians were very numerous in these parts, and had possession of the churches. The members of the Catholic Church were not, however, few in number. They were called Eustathians and Paulinists, and were under the guidance of Paulinus and Meletius, as has been before stated. It was through their instrumentality that the church of Antioch was preserved from the encroachments of the Arians, and enabled to resist the zeal of the emperor and of those in power about him. Indeed, it appears *that in all the churches which were governed by brave men, the people did not deviate from their former opinions*" (*Ecclesiastical History*, bk. 6, chap. 21).

bishop Leontius to the Western bishops[116] and other facts, all of which the anonymous author of the dissertation himself relates, also demonstrate at that time that "The *Ecclesia docens* was the active instrument of the Church's infallibility."[117]

Newman maintained, however, that the hierarchy was not the principle means by which God distinguished the true from the false doctrine. Rather an evolutionary process of natural selection sufficed. "In the earliest age it was simply the living spirit of the myriads of the faithful, none of them known to fame, who received from the disciples of the Lord, and husbanded so well and circulated so widely and transmitted so faithfully, generation after generation, the once-delivered apostolic faith; who held it with such sharpness of outline and explicitness of detail, as enabled even the unlearned instinctively to discriminate between truth and error, spontaneously to reject the very shadow of heresy and to be proof against the fascination of the most brilliant intellects, when they would lead them out of the narrow way."[118]

Newman's concept of merging the role of the laity and the hierarchy in the Church as being indiscriminately responsible for the preservation of the faith seems to have been later adopted in the documents of the Second Vatican Council as follows: "The holy People of God share also in Christ's prophetic office: it spreads abroad

---

116 "They further threatened that they would withdraw from his communion, travel to the Western empire, and publish his plots to the world. Leontius was now alarmed... That excellent pair Flavianus and Diodorus, though not yet admitted to the priesthood and still ranked with the laity, worked night and day to stimulate men's zeal for truth." (*Ecclesiastical History*, bk. 2, chap. 19).

117 Johannes Baptist Franzelin, *Tractatus de divina traditione et scriptura* (Rome, Marietti, 1870), pp. 103-104.

118 *Historical Sketches* (Westminster, Md., Christian Classics, 1970), Vol. 1, pp. 209-10.

a living witness to him, especially by a life of faith and love and by offering to God a sacrifice of praise, the fruit of lips praising his name (cf. Heb. 13, 15). The *whole body of the faithful* who have an anointing that comes from the holy one (cf. I Jn. 2, 20 and 27) cannot err in matters of belief. This characteristic is shown in the supernatural appreciation of the faith (*sensus fidei*) of the whole people, when, from the bishops to the last of the faithful they manifest a universal consent in matters of faith and morals. By this appreciation of the faith, aroused and sustained by the Spirit of truth, the People of God, guided by the sacred teaching authority (*magisterium*) and obeying it, receives not the mere word of men, but truly the word of God (cf. I Thess. 2, 13), the faith once for all delivered to the saints (cf. Jude 3). The People unfailingly adheres to this faith, penetrates it more deeply with right judgment, and applies it more fully in daily life."[119]

Paul Chavasse, the author of "Newman and the Laity," attributes Newman as inspirer of this passage.

This paragraph had originally been intended to form part of Chapter IV, on the laity, but was brought forward into the chapter on the People of God in order to mark the unity that exists between the laity and the hierarchy, which together form the People of God, who cannot err in matters of belief when they show that *universalis consensus* in matters of faith and morals. Objections and amendments to the text, which had wanted to highlight the role of the hierarchy more prominently, were not admitted, because the Council Fathers wanted to show that the *sensus fidei* was not to be considered as a particular prerogative of the hierarchy but as a power of the whole Church. There is a unity in bearing witness to the Faith that belongs to

---

119 *Lumen Gentium*, no. 37.

the totality of the Body of Christ. This concern of the Council Fathers is a most eloquent echo of the *pastorum et fidelium conspiratio* that Newman believed in and advocated so strongly.[120]

How is it that Newman considered the Church teaching practically indistinct from the Church learning? It is because that he had a fundamentally idealistic notion of the Church. For, as Orestes Brownson observed:

Mr. Newman evidently proceeds on the assumption, that Christianity can be abstracted from the Church, and considered apart from the institution which concretes it, as if the Church were accidental and not essential in our holy religion. "Christianity," he says, "though spoken of in prophecy as a kingdom, came into the world as an *idea* rather than an institution, and has had to wrap itself in clothing, and fit itself with armor of its own providing, and form the instruments and methods of its own prosperity and warfare."[121] If he does not so consider it, all he says on the development of ideas in general has and can have no relation to his subject [of the Church].[122]

Hence for Newman the hierarchical structure of the Church was but an evolutionary accretion not originally bestowed upon it by Christ. For, as quoted above, he wrote, "We shall find ourselves unable to fix an historical point at which the growth of doctrine ceased. Not on the day of Pentecost, for St. Peter had still to learn at Joppa about the baptism of Cornelius; not at Joppa

---

120 Paul Chavasse, "Newman and the Laity," in *Newman Today: Papers Presented at a Conference on John Henry Cardinal Newman*, ed. by Stanley L. Jaki (San Francisco, Ignatius Press, 1989).

121 *Development of Doctrine*, p. 77.

122 Orestes Brownson, "Newman's Development of Christian Doctrine," *Brownson Quarterly Review*, vol. 3, n. 3 (July, 1846), pp. 354-355.

and Caesarea, for St. Paul had to write his Epistles; not on the death of the last apostle, for St. Ignatius *had to establish the doctrine of Episcopacy*, not then, nor for many years after, for the canon of the New Testament was still undetermined..."[123] Whereas Pius X condemned the following proposition: "It was far from the mind of Christ to found a Church *as a society* which would continue on earth for a long course of centuries."[124]

---

123 John Henry Newman, *An Essay on the Development of Christian Doctrine* (London, James Toovey, 1845), p. 107.

124 *Lamentabili Sane*, n. 52.

# XI
## *Condemnations Condemned*

Newman not only minimized the role of the Church teaching for the preservation of the faith, he also minimized the authoritative force of its condemnations. For example Pope Pius IX attached a list of condemned liberal propositions with his encyclical, *Quanta cura*. But Newman undermined their authority by raising the doubt whether the pope had himself intended to use his authority in both the encyclical and in the list of propositions. For in *A Letter Addressed to the Duke of Norfolk* he wrote: "The Syllabus is not an official act, because it is not signed [by the Pope]"[125] and "the Syllabus then has no dogmatic force... it is not an exact transcript of the words of the Pope, in its account of the errors condemned."[126]

After minimizing the authority of the Syllabus in general, he then proceeds to minimize the individual condemned propositions:

> For instance, take his own 16th (the 77th of the "erroneous Propositions"), that, "It is no longer expedient that the Catholic Religion should be established to the exclusion of all others." When we turn to the Allocution, which is the ground of its being put into the Syllabus, what do we find there? First, that the Pope was speaking, not of States universally, but of one particular State, Spain, definitely Spain; secondly, that he was not noting the erroneous proposition directly, or categorically, but was protesting against the

---

125 *Certain Difficulties Felt by Anglicans in Catholic Teaching* (London: Longmans, Green and Co., 1900), vol. 2, p. 278.

126 *Ibid,* p. 281.

breach in many ways of the Concordat on the part of the Spanish government... the Pope merely does not think it expedient for every state from this time forth to tolerate every sort of religion on its territory, and to disestablish the Church at once.[127]

The text of the Syllabus as approved by the pope, however, makes no limitation of the domain of the kingship of Christ. All nations, at least in principle, ought to have the Catholic religion as the religion of the state.

Besides the teaching authority of the Church, the teachings of the Church themselves have also evolved according to Newman. For example, he thought that Purgatory and infant baptism evolved out of other seminal teachings of the original revelation given to the Apostles. "Thus we see how, as time went on, the doctrine of Purgatory *was opened upon the apprehension of the Church*, as a portion or form of penance due for sins committed after baptism: and thus the *belief* in this doctrine and the *practice* of infant baptism would *grow* into general reception together."[128] But is this not precisely what Pius X condemned in his Syllabus: "The practice of administering Baptism to infants was a disciplinary evolution, which became one of the causes why the Sacrament was divided into two, namely, Baptism and Penance"?[129]

On these passages of Newman, Orestes Brownson rightly comments as follows: "These passages do not appear in their full strength, detached, as they are, from the context; but we think there is no mistaking the doctrine they inculcate. They prove clearly that Mr. Newman does not mean simply that there has been a growth in theological science, a variation or expansion

---

127 *Ibid,* p. 285.

128 John Henry Newman, *An Essay on the Development of Christian Doctrine* (London, James Toovey, 1845), p. 417.

129 *Lamentabili Sane,* n. 43.

of outward discipline, but that there have been in the teachings of the Church herself real variations of doctrine, an increase and expansion of the Christian creed..."[130] Note here that Pius X condemned the following proposition: "The dogmas the Church holds out as revealed are not truths which have fallen from heaven. They are an interpretation of religious facts which the human mind has acquired by laborious effort."[131]

---

[130] Orestes Brownson, "Newman's Development of Christian Doctrine," *Brownson's Quarterly Review*, vol. 3, n. 3 (July, 1846), p. 350.

[131] *Lamentabili Sane*, n. 22.

# XII
## Evolutionary Doctrinal Development

Since the question of whether Newman's theory of development proposes that the Church independently added specifically new doctrines after Christ to the deposit of faith is critical to this study, we here quote Brownson's thorough analysis of the matter at length. Newman had written in his *Essay on Development of Christian Doctrine*: "... *not in the Creed*, which is no collection of definitions, but a summary of certain *credenda*, an incomplete summary, and, like the Lord's Prayer or the Decalogue, *a mere sample* of divine truths, especially of the more elementary. No one doctrine can be named which starts *omnibus numeris*, at first, and gains nothing from the investigations of faith and the attacks of heresy. The Church went forth from the world *in haste*, as the Israelites from Egypt, 'with their dough before it was leavened, their kneading troughs being bound up in their clothes upon their shoulders.' etc."[132] Whereupon Brownson gave the following commentary:

Now, in regard to all this, we simply ask, Does the Church herself take this view? Does she teach that she at first received no formal revelation, that the revelation was given as "unleavened dough," to be leavened, kneaded, made up into loaves of convenient size, baked and prepared for use by her, after her mission began, and she had commenced the work of evangelizing the nations? Does she admit her original creed was incomplete, that it has increased and expanded, that there have been variation and

---

132 Newman, *An Essay on the Development of Christian Doctrine* (London, James Toovey, 1845), p. 108.

progress in her understanding of the revelation she originally received, and that she now understands it better, and can more readily define what it is than she could at first? Most assuredly not. She asserts that there has been no progress, no increase, no variation of faith; that what she believes and teaches now is precisely what she has always and everywhere believed and taught from the first. She denies that she has ever added a new article to the primitive creed; and affirms, as Mr. Newman himself proves in his account of the Council of Chalcedon, that the new definition is not a new development, a better understanding of the faith, but simply a new definition, against the "novel expressions" invented by the enemies of religion, of what, on the point defined, had always and everywhere been her precise faith. In this she is right, or she is wrong. If right you must abandon your theory of developments; if wrong, she is a false witness for God, and your theory of developments cannot make her worthy of confidence. If you believe her you cannot assert developments in your sense of the term; if you do not believe her, you are no Catholic. This is sufficient to show that Mr. Newman cannot urge his theory as a Catholic, whatever he might do as a Protestant.

Mr. Newman proceeds on the assumption, that the revelation committed to the charge of the Church was not a distinct, formal revelation, but a vague, loose, obscure revelation, which she at first only imperfectly apprehended. This is evident from the extracts we have made, and also from what he says when pointing out an error in a passage which he quotes from one of his previous publications [i.e. editions]. "The writer considers the growth of the doctrine [of Purgatory] an instance of the action of private judgment; whereas

I should now call it an instance of the mind of the Church working out dogmatic truth from implicit feelings, under secret supernatural guidance."[133] This is a pregnant passage, and may be regarded as a key to Mr. Newman's doctrine of development, and also to his view of the teaching authority of the Church. The development, as is evident from the context, is not the formal definition of the faith against a novel error, but is a slow, painful, and laborious working out, by the Church herself, of dogmatic truth from implicit feelings—though what kind of feeling an implicit feeling is, we are unable to say. "Thus St. Justin or St. Irenaeus might be without any digested idea of Purgatory, or Original Sin, yet have an intense feeling, which they had not defined or located, both of the fault of our first nature and of the liabilities of our nature regenerate."[134] It is obvious from the whole course of Mr. Newman's reasoning, that he would predicate of the Church, in their time, what he here predicates of St. Justin and St. Irenaeus. The Church had a vague yet intense feeling of the truth, but had not digested it into formal propositions or definite articles. She had a blind instinct, which, under secret supernatural guidance, enabled her to avoid error and to pursue the regular course of development.[135]

Now it is erroneous to say that the Church originally only had merely a "blind instinct" about the "fault of our first nature." For the *Catholic Encyclopedia* clearly proves the contrary:

---

133 *Ibid*, p. 417.
134 *Ibid*, p. 83.
135 Orestes Brownson, "Newman's Development of Christian Doctrine," *Brownson's Quarterly Review*, vol. 3, n. 3 (July, 1846), p. 352-353.

It is not true that the doctrine of original sin does not appear in the works of the pre-Augustinian Fathers. On the contrary, their testimony is found in special works on the subject. Nor can it be said, as Harnack maintains, that St. Augustine himself acknowledges the absence of this doctrine in the writings of the Fathers. St. Augustine invokes the testimony of eleven Fathers, Greek as well as Latin (*Contra Jul.*, II, x, 33). Baseless also is the assertion that before St. Augustine this doctrine was unknown to the Jews and to the Christians; as we have already shown, it was taught by St. Paul. It is found in the fourth Book of Esdras, a work written by a Jew in the first century after Christ and widely read by the Christians. This book represents Adam as the author of the fall of the human race (vii, 48), as having transmitted to all his posterity the permanent infirmity, the malignity, the bad seed of sin (iii, 21, 22; iv, 30). Protestants themselves admit the doctrine of original sin in this book and others of the same period (see Sanday, *The International Critical Commentary*: Romans, 134, 137; Hastings, *A Dictionary of the Bible*, I, 841). It is therefore impossible to make St. Augustine, who is of a much later date, the inventor of original sin.

That this doctrine existed in Christian tradition before St. Augustine's time is shown by the practice of the Church in the baptism of children... Catholics argued, too, from the ceremonies of baptism, which suppose the child to be under the power of evil, i.e., exorcisms, abjuration of Satan made by the sponsor in the name of the child [Augustine, loc. cit., xxxiv, 63; Denz., n. 140 (96)].[136]

---

136 Harent, Stéphane, "Original Sin. *The Catholic Encyclopedia* (New York, Robert Appleton Company, 1913), vol. 11, p. 313.

Would not Newman's theory of the development of doctrine then fall under the condemned proposition of Pius X: "Dogmas, Sacraments and hierarchy, both their notion and reality, are only interpretations and evolutions of the Christian intelligence which have increased and perfected by an external series of additions the little germ latent in the Gospel"?[137]

Brownson continues: "By the 'mind' of the Church which works out this dogmatic truth, Mr. Newman does not mean, strictly speaking, the constituted authority of the Church, but the internal sense, very nearly what Moehler calls the 'internal tradition,' of the collective body of the faithful. When he speaks of the recipients of the revelation, he seems always to have in his mind the *ecclesia credens*, and to forget the *ecclesia docens*."[138] But Pius X also condemned the proposition: "The 'Church learning' and the 'Church teaching' collaborate in such a way in defining truths that it only remains for the 'Church teaching' to sanction the opinions of the 'Church learning.'"[139]

Brownson rightly warns that this view of the Church teaching would be one of the hierarchy merely rubber stamping the evolutionary teaching molded by the faithful over the course of time:

He does not appear to have ever heard that Almighty God gave his revelation to pastors and teachers qualified from the first to teach it in its purity and integrity, clearly and distinctly—but that he threw it upon the great concourse of believers for them to receive and make the most of. "The time at length came

---

137 *Lamentabili Sane*, n. 54.
138 Orestes Brownson, "Newman's Development of Christian Doctrine," *Brownson's Quarterly Review*, vol. 3, n. 3 (July, 1846), p. 354.
139 *Lamentabili Sane*, n. 6.

when these recipients ceased to be inspired; and on these recipients the revealed truths would fall at first vaguely and generally, and would afterwards be completed by developments."[140] This view, if followed out, would suppress entirely the proper teaching authority of the Church, competent at any moment to declare infallibly what is the precise truth revealed; or, at least, would raise the *ecclesia credens* above the *ecclesia docens*, and reduce the office of the Church teaching to that of defining, from time to time, the dogmatic truth which the Church believing has gradually and slowly worked out from her implicit feelings. The secret supernatural assistance would then attach to the Church believing, and superintend the elaboration, rather than to the Church teaching; and if to the Church teaching at all, only so far as to enable it faithfully to collect and truly define what the Church believing elaborates; the very doctrine we ourselves set forth in the first number of this Review,[141] and insisted on, not as a reason for going into the Roman Catholic Church, but as a reason for not going into it, and for staying where we were.[142]

Owen Chadwick, a non-Catholic authority on Newman's writings, praises Newman from saving the Catholic Church from falling into doctrinal rigidity in modern times as follows:

The new historical studies, the new criticism, might have turned a conservative society towards absolute obscurantism, towards a total rejection of the validity of historical evidence, towards a destruction of the

---

140 *Development of Christian Doctrine*, p. 57.

141 *The Church Question*, Brownson's Works, Vol. IV., p. 461.

142 Orestes Brownson, "Newman's Development of Christian Doctrine," *Brownson's Quarterly Review*, vol. 3, n. 3 (July, 1846), p. 354.

critical doubt by refusing to allow historical inquiry to be relevant to religious faith. Plenty of evidence from the Ultramontism of the middle nineteenth century and after shows that this peril was not imaginary. Greatly to its credit, the conservative community refused to follow several seductive proposals of this kind. To this refusal Newman contributed more than any other Catholic... In the earlier less formed centuries of Christian thinking, ideas of progress and development in religion were not purely intellectual. The soul reaches out to God in faith, and little by little finds the intellectual consequences of what it had felt; and so with the Church. The progress by which this happened is not purely intellectual, but also religious. The later medieval schoolmen, and still more the Spaniards of the Counter-Reformation, wanted to bring clarity into so loose a definition. The only way to make it clearer was to make it a process of the intellect, and not a reaching out in feeling, or in a sort of 'wordless' cognition. Therefore in defining the idea of development, they made it arid. Newman's contribution was not only to develop the idea of development in such a way that history could speak. He brought back feeling, conscience, religious experience, into the process of development. The word *development* was one of the least exciting of all words. Darwin took the word *evolution* and made it speak to the human race. Newman took the word *development* and made it speak to Christendom.[143]

Cardinal Avery Dulles, another modern expert on Newman's writings also detects this same gradual evolutionary theory of doctrinal development in Newman's writings: "He was convinced that Christianity had come

---

143 Owen Chadwick, *From Bossuet to Newman* (Cambridge, Cambridge University Press, 1987), pp. viii-x & xxxi-xxxii.

into the world as a vague global idea, and only gradually found apt expression for itself in dogmatic propositions."[144] Such is nearly the same in Newman's own words: "The theology of the Church is... a diligent, patient, working out of one doctrine out of many materials. The conduct of Popes, Councils, Fathers, betokens the slow, painful, anxious taking up of new elements into an existing body of belief."[145]

But the best authority for analyzing Newman's theory of development of doctrine is once again Orestes Brownson, who made two reviews in his *Brownson's Quarterly*. The first was done in July, 1846, a year after Newman's work, *On the Development of Christian Doctrine*, was first published. In it Brownson is critical but compassionate as he knows that this work was written before his conversion, although Newman edited it and published it after his conversion. But his second review in January 1847 is much less tolerant. This latter article is a book review of Spencer Northcote's book, "The four-fold difficulty of Anglicanism." Northcote had prepared for the priesthood under Newman at Edgbaston and in this article he promotes Newman's theory of development which Brownson assumed that Newman had discarded upon becoming a Catholic. But seeing that Newman was propagating his theory within the Church and forming a group of disciples imbued with the theory, he is obliged to firmly condemn the theory and "to put the faithful on their guard against a work which, under the guise of a defense of our religion, is one of the most insidious attacks, though not so intended by its author, on religion, which we remember to have

---

144 Avery Cardinal Dulles, SJ, "Newman on Infallibility," *Theological Studies*, vol. 51, (1990), n. 4, p. 440.

145 *Development of Christian Doctrine* (London, James Toovey, 1845), p. 353.

ever read."[146] Brownson admits that Newman is capable of being taken out of context but asks his readers to trust his judgment since he knows Newman's theory well from having held it himself before his conversion and from having learned it from Anglican Tractarians themselves. Let us then read his analysis of Newman's theory of development:

Nor are we better satisfied with what Mr. Newman says of the process of development. Christianity came into the world as an idea, an habitual judgment; and we may say of it in particular all he says of development in ideas in general. Ideas, we are told, "are not ordinarily brought home to the mind, except through the medium of a variety of aspects; like bodily substances, which are not seen except under the clothing of their properties and influences, and can be walked round and surveyed on opposite sides, and in different perspectives, and in contrary lights." Let an idea get possession of the popular mind, or the mind of any particular set of persons, and it is not difficult to understand the effects which will ensue.

There will be a general agitation of thought, and an action of mind, both upon itself and upon other minds. New lights will be brought to bear upon the original idea, aspects will multiply, and judgments will accumulate. There will be a time of confusion, when conceptions and misconceptions are in conflict; and it is uncertain whether any thing is to come of the idea at all, or which view of it is to get the start of the others. After a while, some definite form of doctrine emerges; and, as time proceeds, one view of it will be modified or expanded by another, and then combined with a third, till the idea

146 Orestes Brownson, "Newman's Theory of Christian Doctrine," *Brownson's Quarterly Review,* vol. 1 (January, 1847), p. 83.

in which they center will be to each mind separately what at first it was only to all together. It will be surveyed, too, in its relation to other doctrines or facts, to other natural laws or established rules, to the varying circumstances of times and places, to other religions, polities, philosophies, as the case may be. How it stands affected towards other systems, how it affects them, how far it coalesces with them, how far it tolerates when it interferes with them, will be gradually wrought out. It will be questioned and criticized by enemies, and explained by well-wishers. The multitude of opinions formed concerning it, in these respects and many others, will be collected, compared, sorted, sifted, selected, or rejected, and gradually attached to it or separated from it, in the minds of individuals and of the community... Thus, in time, it has grown into an ethical code, or into a system of government, or into a theology, or into a ritual, according to its capabilities; and this system or body of thought, theoretical and practical, thus laboriously gained, will, after all, be only the adequate representation of the original idea, being nothing else than what the very idea *meant* from the first, —its exact image as seen in a combination of the most diversified aspects; with the suggestions and corrections of many minds, and the illustrations of many trials. This process of thought is called the development of an idea.[147]

That this is intended to be a description of the process of development, which takes place in Christian *doctrine*, is evident from the title of the book, *Essay*

---

147 Newman, *Development of Christian Doctrine* (London, James Toovey, 1845), p. 36-37.

*on the Development of Christian Doctrine*, and from what he says expressly:

If Christianity be a fact, and can be made the subject-matter of exercises of the reason, and impress an idea of itself on our minds, that idea will, in the course of time, develop in a series of ideas... It is the peculiarity of the human mind that it cannot take an object in, which is presented to it, simply and integrally. It conceives by means of definition or description; whole objects do not create in the intellect whole ideas, but are, to use a mathematical phrase, thrown into series, into a number of statements, strengthening, interpreting, correcting each other, and, with more or less exactness, approximating, as they accumulate, to a perfect image. There is no other way of learning or of teaching. *We cannot teach, except by aspects or views which are not identical with the thing itself we are teaching* ... And the more claim an idea has to be considered as living, the more various will be its aspects; and the more social and political its nature, the more complicated and subtle will be its developments, and the longer and more eventful will be its course. Such is Christianity; and whatever has been said... about the development of ideas generally becomes, of course, an antecedent argument for its progressive development... Nor is the case altered by supposing that inspiration did for the first recipients of the revelation what the divine fiat did for herbs and plants in the beginning, which were created in maturity.[148] Still, the time at length came when its recipients ceased to be inspired; and on these recipients the revealed truths would fall, as in other cases, at first

---

148 Here we see Newman's use of Butler's *Analogy*.

*vaguely* and *generally*, and would afterwards be completed by developments.[149]

It is plain from this that Mr. Newman means to teach that the Church, in order to attain to an adequate expression of the Christian idea or of Christian doctrine, must institute and carry on the precise process of development which he has predicated of ideas generally; for he contends, and he told us as much in the beginning, that she is forced to do so by the nature of the human mind itself. The revelation is not and cannot be taken in all at once. The Church can neither learn nor teach it, except under particular aspects, none of which, he says, can go the depth of the idea, —that is, we presume, of the fact or no-fact which the idea represents; for it is hardly to be supposed that a judgment cannot go the depth of itself; and it is only by collecting and adjusting these particular aspects, that she can attain to an adequate expression of Christian doctrine. This is naked eclecticism, not in philosophy only, but even in faith.

But this development is effected only gradually, and "after a sufficient time." Some centuries elapse, and the doctrine of Purgatory is "opened upon the apprehension of the Church." She at first cannot take in all revealed truth. She has it all stowed away somewhere, but she only partially apprehends it. As time goes on, as individuals differently circumstanced view it under different particular aspects and from opposite poles, as new controversies arise, bold and obstinate heretics start up, some clamorous for one particular aspect, and some for another, she is able to enlarge her view, to augment the number of her dogmas, and tell us more truly what is the revelation she has re-

149 Newman, *Development of Christian Doctrine* (London, James Toovey, 1845), p. 94-95.

ceived. And this we are to say of a Church we are defending as authoritative and infallible, and which we hold has received the formal commission to teach all nations all things whatsoever Our Lord commanded his Apostles! In plain words, was the Church able to teach truly and infallibly in the age of Saints Clement and Polycarp, or of Saints Justin and Irenaeus, the whole Catholic faith, and the precise Catholic faith, on any and every point which could be made—or was she not? If she was, there can have been no development of doctrine; if she was not, was she not then competent to discharge the commission she received? Was what she then taught the faithful sufficient for salvation? Is not what was then sufficient all that is really necessary now? If so, and if she teaches doctrines now which she did not then or insists on our believing now what she did not then, how will you exonerate her from the charge brought by Protestants, that she has added to the primitive faith, and teaches as of necessity to salvation what is not necessary, and therefore imposes a burden on men's shoulders they ought not to be required to bear? Moreover, where are these developments to stop? Have we reached the end? Has the Church finally brought out the whole body of dogmatic truth, or are we, like the Puritan Robinson, "to look for new light" to break in upon her vision? Mr. Newman seems to think new developments are needed; for he mentions several fundamental matters, which he says he supposes "remain more or less undeveloped, or at least undefined, by the Church."

Mr. Newman, after Leibnitz, represents heresy as consisting in taking and following out a partial view of Christian truth. Will he permit us to ask him to tell us how, at that period, when the Church apprehended the truth only under particular aspects, heresy was distinguishable from orthodoxy? Moreover, if there ever was a time when the Church did not teach the whole faith, how he can maintain her catholicity; since to her catholicity, as we learn from the catechism, it is not only essential that she subsist through all ages, and teach all nations, but that she teach all truth?[150]

In Brownson's second and more severe article on Newman's theory we find the following extract:

The author seems to us, also, to be not quite exact in the following passages.

All Catholic doctrine, as held by the Roman Church, has been the result of one continued law of growth, and has therefore the unity of nature and of life: its development has been like that of the Church itself, 'the least of all seeds, but when it is grown the greatest among herbs'; or, like the growth of grace in each individual soul, "first the blade, then the ear, and after that the full corn in the ear."[151]

The Gospel, it is true, is a divine message. Yet, as the language in which it is made is human, questions may naturally suggest themselves, almost without end, as to the real import of that language; as, for instance, from the brief and mysterious announcement, "the Word became flesh," three wide questions, as it has been well

---

150 Orestes Brownson, "Newman's Development of Christian Doctrine," *Brownson Quarterly Review*, vol. 3, n. 3 (July, 1846), pp. 360-362.

151 James Spencer Northcote, *The Fourfold Difficulty of Anglicanism, Or the Church of England Tested by the Nicene Creed in a Series of Letters* (London, Thomas Richardson and Son, 1846), p. 36.

said,[152] at once open upon us; what is meant by "the Word," what by "flesh," and what by "became"; and inquiries of this kind have, as you know, from time to time arisen in the Church, more or less supported by Scriptural and traditional evidence. These have gradually gained ground and attracted notice, until the Church has felt herself obliged to pronounce judgment upon them, and thenceforward, according to her seal of sanction or anathema, such opinions have either been incorporated into the Catholic Creed, or denounced as contrary to it; and those bodies which, spite of such anathema, have still clung to the proscribed opinions, have gradually become external and hostile to the Church."[153]

This seems to us to teach or necessarily imply— 1. that Christian doctrine grows by virtue of human effort; 2. that a revelation cannot be made through the medium of human language, which shall reach the minds of its recipients in the full and exact sense intended by its author; 3. that heresies arise, as to their matter, from the incompleteness, *quoad se* or *quoad nos*, of the original revelation, and the honest and necessary endeavors of individuals to complete it; and, 4. that opinions may be and are made by the Church articles of faith. There can, it seems to us, be no question that the passages quoted express or imply at least these four propositions, and we should suppose there can be just as little as to their objectionable character.[154]

---

152 Newman, *Development of Christian Doctrine* (London, James Toovey, 1845), p. 97.

153 Northcote, *op. cit.*, pp. 31-32.

154 Orestes Brownson, "Newman's Theory of Christian Doctrine," *Brownson's Quarterly Review*, vol. 1 (January, 1847), pp.

Let us insert here that Saint Thomas Aquinas, on the contrary, taught that the faith was completely and explicitly revealed by Christ to the Apostles, and that new formulations of the faith are merely re-expressions of the faith applied to individual heresies which later arose. For he says, "The truth of faith is sufficiently explicit in the teaching of Christ and the Apostles. But since, according to II Peter 3, 16, some men are so evil-minded as to pervert the Apostolic teaching and other doctrines and Scriptures to their own destruction, it was necessary as time went on to express the faith more explicitly against the errors which arose."[155]

Brownson continues:

Finally, we repeat, from our former article, that we object to the Theory of Developments the very fact that it is a theory. We see no call and no room for theories in the Catholic Church, —least of all, for theories concocted outside of her by men whose eyes are dim, and who have nothing but their own reason to work with.[156] From the nature of the case, they are theories, not for the conversion of their authors, but for the conversion of the Church, —framed to bring her to them, not them to her. They can do no good, and may do much harm. It is natural for us to concoct them when out of the Church, for then we have, and can have, nothing but theories, and can do nothing but theorize; but, if we are wise, we shall not attempt to bring them into the Church with us.

---

42-43.

155 *Summa* II-II, q. 1, a. 10 ad 1[un].

156 Brownson is here referring to Newman's closing paragraph of his *An Essay on the Development of Christian Doctrine* (London, James Toovey, 1845) in which he wrote: "Such were the thoughts concerning the 'blessed vision of peace,' of one, ...while as yet his eye was dim, his breast laden, and he could but employ reason in the things of faith." (p. 453).

The more empty-handed we come to the Church, the better; and the more affectionately will she embrace us, and the more freely and liberally will she dispense to us her graces.

The recent conversion of the author, his evident Catholic intentions, and general soundness of doctrine, would lead us to pass over these points, all uncatholic as they are, with a simple remark calling the attention of our readers to their evident heterodoxy, were they the solitary opinions of Mr. Northcote; but they are the doctrines of a school—of a school formed, indeed, at first outside of the Church, but by the conversion of its distinguished founder, Mr. Newman, and his more eminent disciples, now brought within her communion. Mr. Northcote was one of Mr. Newman's disciples, and the fact that he continues to be one, even within the bosom of the Church, leads us to fear the same may be the case with many others. He gives, in the extracts we have made, what we understand, and what we presume he understands, to be substantially Mr. Newman's doctrine of development. If that doctrine is entertained by the great body of those who have recently abandoned Anglicanism for the Church, the question becomes somewhat grave, and we may have, if we are not on our guard, before we are aware of it, a new school springing up in our midst, as dangerous as the Hermesian or that of De Lamennais. These individuals, from their well-known talents, learning, and zeal, cannot fail to have a wide and commanding influence on our Catholic literature, and, if they adhere to Mr. Newman's doctrine, it will be diffused beyond the circle of those who now entertain it, and do no little harm to portions even of our Catholic population. The age has a strong tendency to theorizing and innovation, which Catholics themselves do not wholly escape. Let there be brought forward a theory which promises to them an opportunity of combining the love of speculation and novelty with reverence for their religion and zeal for the salvation of their neighbor, and the temptation will be too strong to be in all cases successfully resisted. In this view of the question, it becomes important to examine thoroughly Mr. Newman's Theory of Developments, and to lay open to all its real character. If it really authorizes doctrines like those Mr. Northcote sets forth, no Catholic can for a moment, after discovering the fact, entertain it either as true or as harmless...

Mr. Newman's book should have been exempt from Catholic criticism, and would have been, if it had been suffered to pass for what it is and professes to be—the speculations of a man who at best is merely *in transitu* from error to truth. So regarded—it was on its first appearance, and still is by the great body of Catholics at home and abroad, whether of the clergy or the laity—it deserves no censure, and may be read with no inconsiderable interest; for what it contains that is unsound may be justly attributed to the author's former Protestantism, and what is sound may be taken as the concessions of a great and earnest mind to Catholic truth. So regarded, we read the book as it should be read—to find what it contains which we may as Catholics accept, not what it contains which we must reject. But we are compelled to regard it in a different light. Some few within contend the book must needs be orthodox, while those without insist that it is a work from which Catholic faith and theology are to be learned. The very eminence of the author gives weight to the conclusions of both. We are therefore compelled, willing or not, to bring the book to the Catholic standard, and to try it by Catholic principles.

They who, among ourselves, differ from us in our estimate of Mr. Newman's theory, do not, so far as we are informed, differ from us as to the doctrine we oppose to it; but they think that we do not rightly understand it, and ascribe to the author doctrines he would at once repudiate. What Mr. Newman would or would not repudiate, or what he did or did not intend to teach, is not the question we raise; for we review, not him, but his book. What esoteric meaning he may have had we do not inquire. We simply inquire, "What does his book, in the obvious and natural sense of its language, actually teach to plain and unsophisticated readers?" If we have misinterpreted or misrepresented what in this sense it actually teaches, let us be set right or condemned; but if it actually, in the obvious and natural sense of the words used, means what we allege, let it be condemned, whatever hypothesis may or may not be invented to excuse its author. But we trust we may, without offence, entreat those who may be disposed to accuse us of misunderstanding the book, before so accusing us, to take the trouble to read the book themselves, and to be certain that they themselves do not misunderstand it.

Mr. Newman, as is well known, wrote, and in part printed, his essay before he became a Catholic, and, as he personally informed a distinguished friend of ours—if the eminent prelate who is our informant will allow us to call him our friend, who has more than once proved himself to be really so—that he wrote the principal part of it nearly ten years before his conversion. It is not strange, then, nor incredible, that it should not be thoroughly orthodox. Never yet was a Protestant book written that could be converted into a Catholic book;

for, with all deference to Mr. Newman, who maintains the contrary, conversion is not simply taking something in addition to what we before had, but consists in putting off, as well as putting on, in "being *un*clothed," as well as clothed upon. It is not likely the work was commenced with the design with which it was completed; and it requires no very profound examination to discover, that, while the main theory is consistently enough set forth, the book is not all of a piece ; and the hand of the author, retouching it here and there for the press, and striving to give it a more Catholic coloring and expression, is visible enough.[157]

157 Orestes Brownson, "Newman's Theory of Christian Doctrine," *Brownson's Quarterly Review*, vol. 1 (January, 1847), pp. 42-45.

# XIII
## *Mixed Education*

Consistent with his theory of development of doctrine is his supporting of the mixed education of Catholics and Anglicans at the Anglican University of Oxford. For in his mind, the Church of England was merely a group of Christians who had not fully developed their theology into the fully evolved Catholic faith, and consequently he encouraged Catholics to be educated at Oxford. In 1860 Newman opposed the building a new Catholic church in Oxford on the grounds that it might offend the Anglicans there. In a letter to Bishop Ullathorne's secretary, Canon E. E. Estcourt, he explained his reasons at some length:

While I do not see my way to take steps to weaken the Church of England, being what it is, least of all should I be disposed to do so in Oxford, which has hitherto been the seat of those traditions which constitute whatever there is of Catholic doctrine and principle in the Anglican Church... Till things are very much changed there, in weakening Oxford, we are weakening our friends, weakening our own *de facto* [*paidagogos*] into the Church. Catholics did not make us Catholics; Oxford made us Catholics. At present Oxford surely does more good than harm.... There has been a rage for shooting sparrows of late years, under the notion that they are the farmers' enemies. Now, it is discovered that they do more good by destroying insects than harm by picking up the seed. In Australia, I believe, they are actually importing them. Is there not something of a parallel here? I go further than a mere tolerance of Oxford; as I have said, I wish to suffer the Church of England. The Establishment has ever been a breakwater against Unitarianism, fanaticism, and infidelity. It has ever loved us better than Puritans or Independents have loved us.[158]

If one considers but for a moment the number of Catholics persecuted and martyred by the Church of England, one could never accept this strange assertion that the church of murderous Henry VIII and Queen Elizabeth has "ever loved" us Catholics.

Although Newman wished to enroll as many Catholics as possible in the Anglican thinktank of Oxford University, his plan was opposed by the hierarchy and hence he was forbidden to reside at Oxford. Thus, "the Propaganda directed Bishop Ullathorne to 'take heed lest Dr. Newman should do anything which might favor in any way the presence of Catholics at the university.'"[159] Likewise, "Manning, equally alarmed, led the opposition from within the Church. Rallying a number of the bishops behind him, he made representations through his agent, Msgr. Talbot at Rome, that Newman's presence at Oxford would draw many Catholic students to Oxford and further engender 'a certain Anglo-Catholicism' in which the English national spirit would prevail over the Roman and Catholic one."[160]

The Church would naturally have rather favored the establishment of a new Catholic university where Catholics could be safely educated apart from the contagion of heretical sects. But Newman strongly opposed this plan, at least in glorious England. But when "... there was some agitation for the establishment of

---

158 Wilfrid Ward, *Life of Cardinal Newman* (London, Longmans, Green, and Co., 1901), vol. 2, p. 57.

159 John A. O'Brian, *Giants of the Faith* (New York, Image Books, 1960), p. 179.

160 *Ibid.*, p. 178.

a national Catholic university, the cardinal along with other leaders of the Church opposed the project as unwise. 'While I do not wish to speak about what is the best arrangement for other countries, where the conditions are different,' said His Eminence, 'I am certain that for the Church in England the establishments we have at [heretical] Oxford and Cambridge offer the best facilities for Catholic higher education. They are the two great historic centers of intellectual life in England, and our hope is to utilize them more and more. To cut ourselves off from these two great universities and to try to establish a university off by ourselves would be the height of folly, if not positively suicidal. The graduates of Oxford and Cambridge have the ear of the [heretical] English public and are at least listened to with respect.' 'What effect does Oxford have upon the faith of the Catholic students?' we inquired. 'Instead of weakening them,' replied the cardinal, 'we can say now on the basis of a long experience that with the provisions made for them, attending Oxford strengthens them. The graduates of Oxford are supplying the Church with a splendid type of scholarly lay leadership.'"[161]

But mixed education of Catholics and non-Catholics in a non-Catholic school has been disapproved of by the Church. For Pope Leo XIII taught: "Catholics should not choose mixed schools but have their own schools especially for children. They should choose excellent and reputable teachers for them. For an education in which religion is altered or non-existent is a very dangerous education."[162] Again he taught: "It is, then, incumbent on parents to strain every nerve to ward off such an outrage, and to strive manfully to have and to hold exclusive authority to direct the education of their offspring, as is

---

161 John A. O'Brian, *op. cit.*, p. 180.
162 *Militantis Ecclesiae*, Pope Leo XIII, 1897, n. 16.

fitting, in a Christian manner, and first and foremost to keep them away from schools where there is risk of their drinking in the poison of impiety."[163] Likewise the 1917 Code of Canon Law states: "Catholic children may not attend non-Catholic, neutral, or mixed-schools, that is, those which are open also to non-Catholics, and it pertains exclusively to the Ordinary of the place to decide, in accordance with instructions of the Holy See, under what circumstances and with what precautions against the danger of perversion, attendance at such schools may be tolerated."[164]

Schools of higher education are nowise exempt from this prohibition of Canon Law. "Does the provision of canon 1374 apply only to elementary and high schools, or also the colleges and universities? The natural law itself forbids Catholics to attend schools, whatever their grade, if they are dangerous to faith or morals. Both common experience and many documents of the Holy See prove that this danger may exist not only in the elementary and high school but in college and university as well. 'It is almost if not quite impossible for those circumstances to exist which would render attendance at non-Catholic universities free from sin.'[165] It was in regard to universities that the Holy See declared: 'The unformed and unstable characters of young people, the erroneous teaching which is inhaled as it were with the very atmosphere in those institutions without being offset by the antidote of solid doctrine, the great power exerted over the young by human respect and the fear of ridicule on the part of their fellows—all these things produce such a present and proximate danger

---

163 *Sapientiae Christianae*, Pope Leo XIII, 1890, n. 142.

164 CIC 1917 n. 1374.

165 S.C. Prop. Fid., August 6, 1867; *Fontes*, n. 4868, vol. 7, p. 405.

of falling away, that in general no sufficient reason can be conceived for entrusting Catholic young people to non-Catholic universities.'"[166] Clearly then, Cardinal Newman is viewing attendance of Catholic students at the now heretical University of Oxford with Anglicized tinted glasses with little regard to the teaching of the Church on the necessity of Catholic education.

166 *Encyclical of the S.C. Prop. Fid., to the Bishops of England,* 6 Aug. 1867; Fontes, n. 4868, Vol. VII pg. 405; T. Lincoln Bouscaren S.J. and Adam C. Ellis S.J., *Canon Law: A Text and Commentary* (Milwaukee, Bruce Publishing Co., 1957), pp. 744-5.

# XIV
## Anglo-Catholicism versus Catholic Angles

Besides Newman's theory of development, what is more proximately behind Newman's support of Catholics studying at Oxford is his belief that Anglicans are often invisible members of the Catholic Church. The question then is whether his conversion really meant for him the leaving of a heretical body to join the true Church established by Christ, or merely a political shift within the same Church due to his failure to merge the Church of England into the Catholic Church by way of the *via media* of the Oxford movement.

What was the occasion of Newman's conversion? Unlike Manning who left the Church of England amidst great popularity, just four years before his conversion Newman had fallen into disrepute with his Anglican authorities. "Newman's *Tract 90*, 'Remarks on Certain Passages in the Thirty-Nine Articles,' published in January 1841, was designed to demonstrate that the Articles were not the anomaly or difficulty that they might otherwise appear to a 'Catholic Christian.' In a famous passage, Newman claimed that while the Articles were the product of an 'un-catholic age,' they were 'patient' of a 'catholic' interpretation... The outcry was immediate, being heralded by the famous 'Protest of the Four Tutors' at Oxford, and then by the University's Heads of Houses, mainly orchestrated by C. P. Golightly with whom Newman had fallen out. Newman was, in a sense, to be hoisted by his own petard... In fact, opposition to *Tract 90* emanated partly from traditional High Churchmen alarmed at an apparent likeness to an older latitudinarian evasiveness of the Articles that had characterized the anti-subscription campaigners in 1772 and 1835."[167] "There was also the issue that while the *Tract* was really aimed at one group only, his younger 'Romanizing' disciples, it attracted the opprobrium of others...There is no reason to doubt that the negative outcry against the *Tract* from the bishops as well as the Oxford Heads marked the beginning of the end of Newman's life."[168] In fact Meriol Trevor, a modern biographer of Newman, wrote: "Newman was thought a crypto-Roman while he was in the Church of England, as a crypto-Protestant when he was in the Catholic and Roman communion."[169]

The presence of Newman within the Catholic Church was not without some fear about his bringing a Protestantizing influence into the Church. From Rome Msgr. Talbot wrote to Manning: "I am afraid that the *Home and Foreign Review* and the old school of Catholics will rally round Newman in opposition to you and Rome. Stand firm, do not yield a bit in the line you have taken. The Oratory (London) will support you, Ward, and many others, and what is better still, you will have the Holy See on your side... You will have battles to fight, because every Englishman is naturally anti-Roman. To be Roman is to an Englishman an

---

167 Peter B. Nockles, "Oxford Movement," in *The Oxford Handbook of John Henry Newman*, ed. by Frederick D. Aquino and Benjamin J. King (Oxford, Oxford University Press, 2018), pp. 19-20.

168 Peter B. Nockles, "Oxford Movement," in *The Oxford Handbook of John Henry Newman*, ed. by Frederick D. Aquino and Benjamin J. King (Oxford, Oxford University Press, 2018), p. 20.

169 Meriol Trevor, *Newman's Journey* (London, Fontana, 1974), p. 58.

effort. Dr. Newman is more English than the English. His spirit must be crushed."[170]

Manning replied:

Whether he knows it or not he has become the center of those who hold low views about the Holy See, are anti-Roman, cold and silent, to say no more, about the Temporal Power [of the Holy See], national, English, critical of Catholic devotions, and always on the lower side. I see no danger of a Cisalpine Club rising again, but I see much danger of an English Catholicism, of which Newman is the highest type. It is the old Anglican, patristic, literary, Oxford tone transplanted into the Church. It takes the line of deprecating exaggerations, foreign devotions, Ultramontanism, anti-national sympathies. In one word, it is worldly Catholicism, and it will have the worldly on its side, and will deceive many...

Now all these things portend storms, and we shall have them in England. But I have no fear. So long as I know that I have only repeated the words of the Holy See I have no anxiety.

I have not failed to see what you notice in Dr. Newman's pamphlet towards myself, but I do not talk of it, and shall never notice it. The thing which will save us from low views about the Mother of God and the Vicar of our Lord is the million Irish in England, and the sympathy of the Catholics in Ireland. These two things are with anyone who speaks up to the highest note on these two great truths. I am thankful to know that they have no

---

170 Letter of Mrsr. Talbot to Archbishop Manning dated Vatican, February 20, 1866 quoted in E. S. Purcell, *Life of Cardinal Manning, Archbishop of Westminster* (London, MacMillan, 1896), vol. 2, pp. 322-323.

sympathy for the watered, literary, worldly Catholicism of certain Englishmen. It will spread somewhat among the English priests, and will find no little favor among English Jesuits; but the religious of every Order instinctively feel that it is not the mind of the Church. I have, therefore, no great anxiety. It will need much prudence to avoid splits and contradictions among ourselves. But I think we shall do it. Compared with Milner's days, ours are Ultramontane. Even our Anglicanising Catholics are higher than Milner's colleagues.[171]

Newman, however, complained to Msgr. Talbot about his criticizing of himself, to which Talbot replied:

I do not deny that certain expressions in your later writings have not pleased me, and that I could not approve of certain acts of yours which had the appearance of being opposed to the wishes of the Holy See.

Besides, a certain school in England have done you much harm by making many believe that you sympathized with their detestable views. You have also been more injured by your friends than your enemies. When I was in England three years ago, I heard some of them quoting your name in opposition to the Authority of the Holy See. I remarked that there was a party forming of what are called 'Liberal Catholics,' who wished to place you at their head, in preference of professing a filial devotion to the Vicar of Christ, and a due veneration for the Chair of St. Peter.

There is a saying: "God defend me from my friends; I can defend myself from my enemies."

Such is your case. For twenty years I was your warm admirer and defender, and should be delighted to be

---

171 Letter dated 25 Feb. 1866, quoted in E. S. Purcell, *Life of Cardinal Manning, Archbishop of Westminster* (London, MacMillan, 1896), vol. 2, pp. 322-4.

so still, but when I found that there was a dangerous party rising in England, who quoted your name, I was obliged to modify my views, and stand up for Ecclesiastical Authority in preference of worshipping great intellectual gifts.[172]

172 Wilfrid Ward, *Life of Cardinal Newman* (London, Longmans, Green, & co., 1912), p. 178.

# XV
## *Publicly Controverted*

To summarize the two opposite views of Newman, either as a pre-modernist or as a loyal defender of the Catholic faith, let us see how the Catholic journals of his time opposed each other in their assessment of the ideas he brought with him into the Church from various non-Catholic sources.

The most blunt, perhaps, of all the reviews appeared anonymously in *The Edinburgh Review*. This writer quoted passages from Tyrrell, Edouard LeRoy, and the Italian clerical authors of *The Programme of Modernism*, asserting that although Newman would have been horrified at these modernists' conclusions, he had in fact laid down the very principles which they logically drew out. "Although Newman was not a Modernist, but an exceedingly stiff conservative," says the writer, "he did introduce into the Roman Church a very dangerous and essentially alien habit of thought which has since developed into Modernism.... One side of his religion was based on principles which, when logically drawn out, must lead away from Catholicism in the direction of an individualist religion of experience, and a substitution of history for dogma which makes all truth relative and all values fluid. [Newman's writings have always made genuine Catholics uneasy, though they hardly know why. It is probable that here is the solution.]"[173] Whether or not one agrees with that assessment of Newman, one must admit that it sets in bold relief the real issues

---

173 "Cardinal Newman," *The Edinburgh Review*, vol. 215, no. 440 (April 1912): pp. 288-289.

at stake in the Newman-modernist controversy, and it honestly juxtaposes the Roman Catholic theological structure as it presented itself to the world at the turn of this century with those Roman Catholics who in one way or another were challenging the rigidity and narrowness of that structure.

The challenge of the *Edinburgh Review* writer was taken up at once by the English Jesuit journalist Father Sydney Smith who wrote at length in the Jesuit periodical *The Month*. While Smith ostensibly dealt with the Edinburgh writer's arguments point by point, he did so on the basis of an unarticulated assumption which became the standard Roman Catholic platform in this matter down to our own day. And that assumption is that what Newman really meant, when he spoke of such things as evidence and belief or of conscience and authority, was exactly what the scholastic expositors of official Roman Catholic doctrine in the nineteenth century meant by those terms. Anyone, for instance, who knows of Newman's lifelong relationship with the agnostic William Froude, of the many lengthy and carefully thought-out letters he wrote to Froude, and of the importance of Froude's experience to Newman's argument in the *Grammar of Assent*, knows that Smith's assumption is a false one. Smith concluded his article, apparently aware that the intrinsic cogency of his argument was inadequate, by quoting Pius X's defense of Newman against the modernists, and by asserting that the Edinburgh writer was 'ill-qualified to judge on such a question.'[174] In other words, authority, not reason and evidence, was to settle the question of Newman's relationship to Modernism.

---

174 Sydney F. Smith, "Newman's Relation to Modernism," *The Month*, vol. CXX, no. 577 (July 1912): p. 15.

The elaboration of and response to the question of whether Newman was a modernist in our second sense, from the publication of Ward's biography down to our own day, has been full and circuitous. Even to mention the most important twists and turns in the argument over the past eighty years would require a book, and there is no time now to do more than mention several of the most recent articles on this point.

Until about thirty years ago modernist scholarship was in a wasteland, with only Alec Vidler's *The Modernist Movement in the Roman Church* of 1934 standing between general Roman Catholic rejection of the modernists and non-Catholic general indifference toward them. Since the Second Vatican Council, however, interest in the modernists for their own sake and interest in their relationship to Newman has revived. In 1971 Doctor B. M. G. Reardon of the University of Newcastle upon Tyne published an article on "Newman and the Catholic Modernist Movement" in which he suggested that although Newman would have been appalled at the conclusions of Loisy, Tyrrell, and others; still, Newman's approach to faith, his sense of the relationship of doctrine to life, and above all, his understanding of the necessity of a theory of doctrinal development, all at one or another point touch ideas and theories developed by and condemned in the modernists.[175]

Here is a sample passage from the above-mentioned scalding *Edinburgh Review* which summarizes Newman's

---

175 Lawrence Barmann, "Theological Inquiry in an Authoritarian Church: Newman and Modernism," in *Discourse and Context : An Interdisciplinary Study of John Henry Newman*, ed. by Gerard Magill (Carbondale, Southern Illinois University Press, 1993), pp. 186-188.

skeptical view that because religious truths cannot be adequately known by men, they cannot be infallibly taught by the Church.

And yet, when Newman pours scorn upon human reason, and when he enthrones the "conscience" as the supreme arbiter of truth, is he not, in fact, preparing the way for these startling declarations, which imply a complete rupture with Catholic authority? Dogmas are indisputably "notional" propositions; that is to say, they belong to that class of truths to which Newman ascribes only a very subordinate importance. We cannot, in his sense, "assent" to an historical proposition as such, but only to the authority which has ordered us to believe it. And is there any justification for Newman's confidence that this authority may make apparent innovations, such as he admits to have been made throughout the history of the Church, but no real changes? If he had been able to think out the implications of his doctrine of development with the help of such arguments as those of Bergson, would he not have seen that without change and real innovation there can be no true evolution? Do not the fluidity and pragmatic character of dogma, so much insisted on by Sabatier and Le Roy, follow from the anti-intellectualist personalism which we have seen to be the foundation of Newman's philosophy of religion? The Modernist might argue that he is only extending to the history of the Church the doctrine of education by experience which Newman found to be true in the life-history of the individual.[176]

---

176 "Cardinal Newman," *Edinburgh Review*, vol. 215, n. 440 (April, 1912), p. 286

# *Conclusion*

To conclude it is not sufficient to take liberal or orthodox quotations from the writings of Newman, for both can be found and some even directly contradicting one another. Newman was willing to submit to Church authority at least externally, which saves him from any ecclesiastical censure. He is elusive, and probably deliberately so, to avoid any direct confrontation with his superiors. Before the condemnation of Modernism, Newman can be given more leeway in proposing ideas that when fully developed can be classified as modernistic. We can excuse the man but not his ideas which knowingly or unknowingly infected the Church with foreign, liberal principles which later burst out at the Second Vatican Council, infecting nearly the whole Church with the contagious plague of Modernism. One can attempt to save both Newman and Vatican II with a dreamy slogan of seeking a "hermeneutic of continuity," but only if one is willing to naively follow popular opinion and not carefully investigate the actual writings of both. Rather let us then reverse Newman's motto, *Ex umbris et imaginibus in veritatem*,[177] such that we begin with the light of revealed Truth to correctly judge what is uncertain human knowledge, as opposed to skeptically attempting to base our knowledge of revelation upon the weak foundation of fallible human perceptions. *Lux Veritatis dispellit umbram dubii.*[178]

---

177 I. e., "Out of shadows and phantasms into the truth."
178 I. e., "The Truth dispels the shadow of doubt."

# Appendix I

## Extract from *Tractatus de Sacra Doctrina*[179]
### *by* Alexis Cardinal Lepicier

ARTICLE IV. *Whether it is permitted to expect a new interpretation of handed down revelation either from the natural sciences or from the elaboration of the Christian conscience.*

**1.—Figments of the Modernists' imagination—** Since we have already seen above that many of the Modernists have endeavored that a change in Catholic dogma be introduced, both on the part of the dogma itself[180] and also on the part of the extension of Christian revelation,[181] now the theories come to be considered of those who want movements of change of the interpretation of dogma to be undertaken, so that in fact the same formulas be allowed a different interpretation according to different times and circumstances.—Now their theories can be suitably reduced to two main points: namely, either it may be said, with the advancement of the natural sciences, the notion of the faith, which proportionally corresponds with them, ought to be enlarged; or that Catholic dogma, suitably elaborated by the Christian conscience, is subject to perpetual transformation.

**2.—The system of those saying that the knowledge of the faith, ought to be proportionally enlarged with the natural sciences—** And indeed regarding the

---

179 Rome, Buona Stampa, 1927), P. 263-317.
180 Art. 1.
181 Art. 2 & 3.

first, just as by the exercise of the human intelligence, we see new theories of the positive sciences daily increasing, so those who devise new things, let themselves be elated with a seductive hope, that the day is not far off when with more and more advanced natural sciences, new formulas of faith, besides, not contrary to, the dogmas received up until now, are to be proposed to the human race. Surely there is an intimate connection between the natural and supernatural orders; hence it is impossible, they say, with the growing knowledge of the former order, that an increase of truths of the latter order would not follow; and so, having now increased the number of discoveries of the positive sciences and the natural truths having received increases, it ought to be expected that with due study many new truths of this supernatural order, with the passing of time, be discovered.

**3.—The system of this kind refuted**—We certainly admit that a certain analogy ought to be kept between both orders, but not a perfect likeness, and hence it follows that not everything that is said about one order can be extended to the other. Indeed, in both orders it is found that because both immediately proceed from God, and God's works are perfect, it follows that both, as much as its nature permits, turned out perfect: wherefore both the work of the six days was perfect and the Church came forth perfect from the side of the dying Redeemer. And this perfection truly prevailed not only in the real order but also in the logical order; for Adam had been formed immediately by God, and had been endowed with the knowledge of all truths, both natural and supernatural, that pertained to him: and yet he would not transmit it to his posterity in this way, since only he was the head and instructor of the whole human race.

But when original sin supervened, the darkness of ignorance covered the minds of Adam and of his posterity: not in such a way that Adam actually lost all of either the natural or supernatural knowledge infused into himself, but certainly in the sense that these truths, especially what pertains to the supernatural order, having in fact already been somewhat obscured in Adam himself, were more feebly received by his offspring, and with the passing of time, were transmitted still more imperfectly from father to son.

Wherefore, also, as to what pertains to natural truths, man had to labor much to obtain them again for himself, through many periods of errors, finally arriving at that possession of philosophical truths, which, for example, we see obtained in Aristotle. Since, however, supernatural truths are those which man is unable to acquire by himself, hence their knowledge having nearly completely corrupted with the passing of time, it was necessary that God would once more reveal them to man: which happened inchoately in fact under the Patriarchs and the Law of Moses, but fully by Christ, His only begotten Son: and precisely because these truths completely surpass the grasp of the human mind, it follows that they all had to be revealed by God, although, from these same revealed truths man could deduce many things for knowing more deeply and embracing more firmly the supernatural order.

Therefore, the Church was so founded by Christ and propagated by the Apostles in such a way that it was from the beginning in full possession of revelation; even though supernatural truths were due to be still more explicitly known and more elucidated with course of time.

4.—**Tacit objection solved**—And it ought not to be said that the ancient Christians were too ignorant to be able to bear such sublime doctrine: for Our Lord did

not promise in vain that He would give the Holy Ghost
to the faithful, Whom they needed so that their hearts
might be enlightened: hence although the Apostles had
firstly heard from Christ: "I have yet many things to say
to you: but you cannot bear them now,"[182] afterwards,
namely when Christ had already ascended into heaven,
"They were all filled with the Holy Ghost, and they
began to speak with divers tongues, according as the
Holy Ghost gave them to speak."[183]

"5.—**Error of the Modernists concerning the evolution of dogma elaborated in the Christian conscience**.—After having thus established these things,
it is easy for us to discuss that fiction of the Modernists,
seeking a new interpretation, or as they say, an evolution, of Catholic dogma, from the elaboration of the
Christian conscience, assuredly by the working of the
Holy Ghost, as they say.

Certainly, not all Modernists accept that the evolution of this kind ought to be attributed to the Holy
Ghost, since many seem to even abhor naming the Holy
Ghost, very many of them also would probably reply to
anyone asking what is the Holy Ghost, by that saying
of the disciples of Ephesus: "We have not so much as
heard whether there be a Holy Ghost."[184] —Therefore
we can put aside those men who put the progress of
the knowledge of dogma solely in the bare evolution of
the Christian conscience: since their system, founded in
mere vital immanence, has been sufficiently refuted in
the encyclical *Pascendi Dominici Gregis*.

Thus, the opinion of those who propose that the evolution of this kind is due to the Holy Ghost, working not

---

182 Jn. 16, 12.
183 Acts 2, 4.
184 Acts 19, 2.

by His gifts, but immediately in the intimate conscience of each man, is more subtle and destructive.

**6.—Foundation of this error**—The foundation of this error is found in the teaching of the Americanists[185] who, having followed the opinions of Isaac Thomas Hecker, were arguing that the time had come for a new and much broader internal action of the Holy Ghost in the Church. Although in times past the assertion of an exterior authority, against the Protestants, seemed more necessary, this authority ought to now make way for the interior impulse of the Holy Ghost, immediately leading each and every man by himself to the truth. Leo XIII explains this teaching along with the other errors of the Americanists as follows: "All external guidance is set aside for those souls who are striving after Christian perfection as being superfluous or indeed, not useful in any sense—the contention being that the Holy Ghost pours richer and more abundant graces than formerly upon the souls of the faithful, so that without human intervention He teaches and guides them by some hidden instinct of His own."[186]

Therefore, in the first place it ought to be supposed, as they say, that the beginning of all progress in the knowledge of dogma, is based upon some innate need

---

185 A certain priest named Andrew Towianski preceded the Americanists, who can be called the founder, not to say precursor, of the more recent enlightened men who do not hesitate to call themselves the *Cavalry of the Holy Ghost*. His works, in which completely foreign doctrines were defended, have already been condemned by the Index, on April 21, 1850.—To this matter the condemnation of the Holy Office issued on August 20, 1894, of the three American societies can be referred, namely the Odd Fellows, the Sons of Temperance, and the Knights of Pythia (Acta Leonis XIII, vol. 14, p. 292).

186 Letter *Testem bonevolentiae*, to the Archbishop of Baltimore, Jan. 22, 1899 Acta Leoni XIII, v. 19, p. 11.

of the subject, to which corresponds a certain internal feeling; and hence having supposed that faith in God and Divine things ought to be referred to this internal feeling of a welled-up need or desire for the Divinity, it then ought to be concluded that all evolution or progress in the knowledge of Catholic dogma ought to be attributed to the operation of the Holy Ghost, immediately stirring up this special need or desire and this internal feeling in the soul,[187] so that in this way a certain new interpretation may be given to consecrated formulas.

**7.—The Logical Consequences from the aforesaid suppositions**—Now it is befitting that the things which logically follow from thence, and which are moreover accepted by the Modernists, be treated with a few words. Firstly, what in reality pertains to revelation in general, they explain as nothing other than man's acquired consciousness of his relation to God,[188] to the extent that the notion of the relation of this kind is acquired in the consciousness elaborated from the aforesaid criteria. Next, the dogma which the Church proposes as revealed truth, ought not to be taken as truths fallen from heaven or announced; but they are a kind of interpretation of religious facts, which the human mind prepared for itself by a laborious effort.[189] Now to one asking whence comes forth the doctrine which Paul, John, and the Council of Nicaea hand down about Christ's Divinity, and which the faithful retain, the answer will be given, that this is not the very same teaching which Jesus taught, but what the Christian conscious conceived about Jesus.[190] Hence also the facts

---

187 Cf. Encycl. *Pascendi*, shortly after the beginning.
188 Decree *Lamentabili*, prop. 20 (Dz. 2020).
189 *Ibid*, Prop. 22 (Dz. 2022).
190 *Ibid*, Prop. 27 and 31 (Dz. 2027 & 2031).

narrated in the Gospels, and especially the Savior's Resurrection, are not properly facts of the mere supernatural order, nor demonstrated or demonstrable, but gradually derived from other sources.[191]—Lastly, regarding what generally pertains both to the notion and the reality of the dogmas, of the Sacraments, and of the hierarchy, it ought to be said that these things are nothing other than interpretations and evolutions of the Christian intelligence by which the little germ latent in the Gospel is augmented and perfected.[192]

As is apparent to one carefully considering, positions of this kind make one thing clear, namely that every single man, by the labor of his internal conscience, forms and fashions to himself, according to his own manner, and under the influence of the Holy Ghost, the notion both of the revelation in general, and of every single doctrine in particular: such that our knowledge of doctrine can be called the offspring of our own mind, in the sense that not only the first desire of this knowledge is in us from the Holy Ghost, but also every effort by which we attain to this knowledge, and also the attaining itself, without it being necessary for the perception of the mind to turn towards outward things.

**8.—Proposition—The system of the elaboration of conscience ought to be rejected.**

**9.—Authority**—In the first place, the solemn passage of Saint Paul contradicts this modernistic figment of the imagination: "Faith cometh by hearing; and hearing by the word of Christ."[193] Doubtless, as the Angelic Doctor explains: "Two dispositions concur in the virtue of faith; first, the habit of the intellect whereby it is disposed to obey the will tending to Divine truth. For the intellect

---

191 *Ibid*, Prop. 36 (Dz. 2036).
192 *Ibid*, Prop. 54 (Dz. 2054).
193 Rom. 10, 17.

assents to the truth of faith, not as convinced by the reason, but as commanded by the will; hence Augustine says, 'No one believes except willingly.' In this respect faith comes from God alone. Secondly, faith requires that what is to be believed be proposed to the believer; which is accomplished by man, according to Romans 10, 17: 'Faith cometh by hearing...'; principally, however, by the Angels, by whom Divine things are revealed to men."[194]

**10.—Theological Reason**—Next, it ought to be observed that the Holy Ghost in the propagation of the faith, as in all works of grace and nature, so proceeds such that He keeps the order of secondary causes as far as possible, since, to be concise, the species of effects is determined by their secondary causes, and except by a miracle, the order of the secondary causes may never be set aside: the propagation of the faith, however, is not a miracle. Therefore, if the immediate cause of the knowledge of revelation were to be the need of the subject and that interior perception, since things of this sort will vary in each individual, it will be impossible that unity in revelation and doctrine may be had: for unity is not taken from the remote principle, but proximate principle, just as the unity of plants is not taken from the sun which is only the remote cause of the vegetation, but from the specific difference of the seeds: and indeed specific unity is lacking in plants precisely because every plant has its own proper cause, which is a seed specifically distinct from the seeds of other plants. Since therefore in every man there are both different needs and perceptions or instincts, then there ought to also be in every man an apprehension of revelation and dogmas in the revelation of the contents, if indeed the beginning of our knowledge of the truths of the faith would have been taken from the aforesaid need to be

---

194 I, q. 111, art. 1 ad 1[um].

fulfilled under the immediate operation of the Holy Ghost.—Certainly from this error that most pernicious error of our present time has spread, every religion is good and of itself leads man to happiness, as long as one does not refuse to faithfully follow its dictate.[195]

But, given also that the need and perception of each individual man are equal, how can we become more certain, that the attempt of the conscience to obtaining that to which our instinct is led, is conformed not merely to natural reason, but also to the supernatural order? Certainly it ought to be known to everyone, that due to Original Sin a bitter fight against reason was left in the lower faculties of the soul, according to that passage of Saint Paul: "But I see another law in my members, fighting against the law of my mind, and captivating me in the law of sin, that is in my members."[196] But, even if there were perfect harmony of the senses with reason, actually revelation and whatever pertains to the supernatural order surpasses the capacity of nature to such an extent that it is incapable of making even the least desire in that order, according to the saying of Saint Paul: "Eye hath not seen, nor ear heard, neither hath it entered into the heart of man, what things God hath prepared for them that love him" (I Cor. 2, 9). Certainly that sense is completely incapable, the root of which hides in the subconsciousness according to the Modernists, of eliciting even the least desire for things pertaining to the supernatural order; furthermore this sense, even in regard to those things which pertain to the natural order, needs to be regulated and moderated by reason, since of itself it is blind and tends to evil.

"This need of the divine, which is experienced only in special and favorable circumstances, cannot, of itself,

---

195 Cf. Syllabus of Pius IX, prop. 15-18.
196 Rom. 7, 23.

appertain to the domain of consciousness; it is at first latent within the consciousness, or, to borrow a term from modern philosophy, in the SUBCONSCIOUSNESS, where also its roots lie hidden and undetected."[197]

**11.—The concept of the false conscience**—Finally it ought to be observed, the concept of conscience is razed to the ground by the Modernists, to which they attribute the role of elaborating doctrine and the knowledge of doctrine: although according to the principles of sound philosophy, the word *conscience*, derived from the words *cum alio scientia*, [i.e. knowledge applied to an individual case], properly signifies the application of the practical knowledge which we possess to our actions, according to which conscience in us either testifies that we have done or not done something, or judges that something ought to be done or omitted, or decides that something that has been done was done correctly or incorrectly, in which sense it is sometimes said to excuse, accuse, or torment, i.e. reprehend.[198] Yet because the act of conscience proceeds as from a principle, from the natural habit of the first moral principles which is called *synderesis*, to which corresponds the *understanding of principles*, which is the natural habit of the first speculative principles; hence by a synecdochical figure, whereby the effect is named for the name of the cause, the conscience itself is sometimes is called synderesis, or the natural judicator, or the law of our intellect.[199] But nowise can the labor of the mind investigating speculative truth be attributed to the conscience.

**12.—The foundation of the system of the elaboration of the Christian conscience**—Now in order

---

197 Encyclical *Pascendi*, n. 7.
198 Cf. I, q. 79, a. 13.
199 *Ibid.*

that the falsity of the system which we are fighting against, according to which *the religious sentiment, which by vital immanence breaks forth from the hidden recesses of the subconsciousness, the germ of the all religion, and likewise the explanation of everything which was or will be in any religion,*[200] it will be helpful to briefly repeat what are the foundations on which the audacious attempt of the Modernists rests. Without a doubt there are these two, namely the evolutionist Spencer and the subjectivist Kant; and in fact that neediness pertains to Spencerian evolutionism whereby the subject is stimulated to accepting new points of doctrine; but to Kantian subjectivism ought to be referred that religious sentiment, which having been manifested in the conscious, excites it to elaborating doctrines unto oneself.—We confidently say, in all the works of the Modernists, one always detects traces of these two elements, because they draw, directly or indirectly, from the aforesaid English or German philosophers, having neglected the more sound scholastic philosophy.

And firstly, as to what pertains to Spencer, it is certainly known that he extended to religion the principles which Darwin applied to the physical, moral and social orders, such that the religious sentiment and every form of religion, according to him, ought to be said to have evolved from a primal need of nature.[201] Now the Modernists have attempted to discover the manner of this evolution in the principles of Kant: certainly since, according to this German philosopher, phenomena in this ought to be distinguished from noumena, because the former represent a certain sensible perception, as the

---

200 Encyclical *Pascendi*, n. 10.

201 How more recent evolutionists draw the origin of religions from the principles of transformism, we have set forth in the book, *L'opera dei sei giòrni*, P. II, c. VII, p. 263. Firenze, 1904.

material element of our thoughts, the latter, however, represent the objective reality itself, as the formal element innate to our mind *a priori*, hence knowledge is completed, according to which the latter *a priori* form is applied to the element furnished by the senses. On this point the idealism of Rosmini ought to be recalled, to which all systems of subjectivist philosophers can be ultimately reduced.—According to this system, a certain external process of events and changes will be had in the Church: but that interpretation of all these things will be given which each one shall have elaborated according to the idea that has arisen within himself, or begotten unto himself: now the two aforesaid agents, namely need and interior sentiment, according to the more scrupulous Modernists, ought to be said to have been derived from the Holy Ghost.

**13.—Figments of the Modernists' imagination—** It will be clearer why from these erroneous principles the whole Modernistic pestilence comes forth if we bring forth only a few things from their writings. Certainly, to someone firstly asking what faith is, they reply that it is nothing other than life itself lived Christianly, which through intellectual elaboration, conformed to various philosophical categories of different times, gave the origin to different and successive formulas.

Wherefore, they say, the Christian religion takes α) from Stoicism the precepts and formulas of the highest morality; β) from Platonic philosophy and Aristotelian syllogistic figures (*schemata*) both the impulsion relative to the evolution of doctrine and applying formulas; γ) from the Roman Empire the hierarchic and constitutional element; lastly δ) from Christ's Semitic mind the new revelation of the relation of man to God, that is, the notion of Divine Paternity.—Hence, they say, it does not belong to the Church to authoritatively interpret doc-

trine, since it belongs to it merely to offer fitting formulated expressions of the doctrines which the faithful receive, by taking conscience from them and attributing a
personal and subjective meaning to them. Hence, when
some formulated expression is now no longer suitable
for expressing the new emotion or religious sentiment
of some determinate epoch, it ought to be modified. Now
regarding the fundamental truth of God's existence, the
arguments derived from the principle of causality are
worthless: the only valid argument is the Kantian moral
argument. Finally, so that I may omit many things, the
argument in favor of the Christian religion is relative,
and does not have anything objective in it, to which absolute, perfect and universal value can be attributed.

Briefly, to someone asking how the progress in faith
was had with the passing of time, the answer will be
given than *vital evolution brought with it progress... not
by the accretion of new and purely adventitious forms
from without, but by an increasing penetration of the
religious sentiment in the conscience.* [202]

**14.—How the Modernists reconcile the elab-
oration of conscience with the exercise of authority.**— Next, since numerous efforts of Modernism
ultimately aim at this, namely that they completely de-
bilitate the force of the authority Divinely constituted in
the Church, although the innovators do not call for this
to be immediately taken away, but they concede that it
ought to be endured as long at the Church herself shall
have been induced to sanction that which the Christian
conscience asks from her.

Certainly, as they say, between the authority and
the consciences of individual persons there is a certain
consensus by an agreement, that firstly indeed the consciences of individual persons flow together into the col-

---

202 Encyclical *Pascendi*, n. 26.

lective conscience, but this [flows together] unto men exercising authority, until it forces them to sanction [the collective conscience] with their approval. It is indeed hardly possible that formulas, whereby dogma have been expressed up until now would immediately change: yet they are sure that it will be done sometime, namely when the collective conscience has sufficiently evolved. For the present time then the received formulas ought to be upheld, yet such that the formulas themselves are distinguished from that which is contained by the formulas. For the Church receives from learned men and consecrates for a time some formula chosen and worked out by them, such as the word *transubstantiation*, as more opportune for the present time; the role of the faithful, however, is not to adhere to the formulas, but that they try to attain to the unknown, which symbolically, albeit very imperfectly, is represented in the aforesaid formulas. Therefore, once it has been established that some formula is inadequate for representing the Divine concept or for expressing the new sentiment of the faithful, it ought to then give way to another formula.

Now because the Modernists consequently in fact acknowledge that change of this kind can only occur slowly, they thence indeed proclaim the necessity of being wary of inconsiderate impulses whereby the work of transformation can be completely destroyed. Hence, they say, the function of the constituted authority is to moderate the elaboration of the collective conscience: hence they admit to be submissive to it with exterior, but not interior, compliance, insofar as it is necessary that individual men remain within bounds of the Church, so that the collective conscience may, with men simultaneously united together, gradually be changed. But, if the authority in the meantime exercises his office by plucking off the leaders of Modernism, they nevertheless are encouraged by the consciousness of having acted rightly: hence *they reflect that, after all there is no progress without a battle and no battle without its victim, and victims they are willing to be like the prophets and Christ Himself.*[203]

**15.—Comments—** I. Who does not see how abusively the sacred office of ecclesiastical authority is dishonored here? To it certainly does not belong the office, as it has been maintained until now, according to Christ's promise of leading the way, of indicating the path of truth, and of commanding that all men go by this path: but as a humble pedestrian, it traces the footprints of the sentiment of popular progress, instructed by it, and finally whatever things there may be, it makes sacred and consecrates. Now what about prelates constituted in authority? They, especially the Roman pontiff, are not pastors who lead the sheep to healthy pasture, warding away from poisonous pasture; but are at most dogs following the flock, circling around it barking, lest erratic sheep wander away.—What clearer perversion can be given to the doctrine of Christ and of the Fathers?

II. Now because we make mention of authority, we cannot but be inflamed with anger by those writers, who do not wish to perchance be called non-Catholics, and yet miss no occasion of disparaging the prelates of the Church: to whom assuredly that passage of Exodus can be applied: "A beast shall touch the mount, it shall be stoned,"[204] and also that which is read in the Second Book of Kings,[205] namely Oza was struck by the Lord, because he touched the ark of the covenant; by a

---

203 Encyclical *Pascendi*, n. 27.
204 Ex. 19, 13, quoted according to Heb. 12, 20.
205 II Kings 6, 7.

mountain and by the ark the legitimate prelates of the Church are signified.[206]

**16.—How far the aforesaid system of elaboration of the Christian conscience is from the doctrine of St. Augustine concerning the seminal notions**—Now because it seems to not a few that the very famous opinion of the Doctor of Hippo[207] concerning the seminal notions of things is akin to the Modernistic system which we have now attacked, in regard to the Christian conscience elaborating unto itself the symbol of faith, it will help here to make a comparison between both teachings, so that the falsity of that Modernistic blemish may appear more, and contrariwise the Catholic truth may shine forth more brilliantly.

Thus St. Augustine posited that the world was so created by God in the beginning that each species of things existed in potency and not in act, so that in it seeds of all things would exist, to be developed in the course of time.[208] To this position regarding cosmology, the holy Doctor added another pertaining to ideology: according to which the concepts are in our mind also as the seeds of all things to be known.—Certainly this opinion of Augustine, borrowed from Plato, with whose teaching he was imbued, could perhaps absolutely speaking, meaning as it sounds materially, be taken in a Modernistic sense: but, as St. Thomas expounds, it ought to be explained in another sense, which is actually conformed to the mind of the Doctor of Hippo, namely that there is present in man an innate aptitude

---

206 "It would seem that a subject touches his prelate inordinately when he upbraids him with insolence, as also when he speaks ill of him: and this is signified by God's condemnation of those who touched the mount and the ark." (II-II, q. 33, a. 4 ad 1$^{um}$)

207 I.e. St. Augustine of Hippo.

208 We have expounded this opinion of St. Augustine in the book, *L'opera dei sei giòrni*, P. I, c.VI.

for correctly knowing the first principles, both speculative and practical. Now a certain ability in the supernatural order corresponds to this natural aptitude, derived from the virtue of faith, for perceiving the mysteries contained in revelation.

Now from the gifts of the intellect, of wisdom and knowledge, as we saw, arises in man a certain Divine sense and savoring of things of the faith, and also a certain delight concerning the revealed mysteries, along with a desire for knowing further things: hence as philosophy has arisen from the desire of knowing natural things, so sacred theology has arisen from the desire for knowing supernatural things, which precisely endeavors to laying open [*evolvenda*] the seeds of the faith. Hence concerning wisdom it is said: "She preventeth them that covet her, so that she first sheweth herself unto them... For the beginning of her is the most true desire of discipline."[209] Therefore it ought to be understood in this sense what St. Augustine has written in various places concerning the seminal reasons applied to the supernatural order.

**17.—Authoritative declarations concerning this matter**—How no interpretation is to be expected of new dogmas of the faith, nay the possibility of attributing a new meaning to the dogmas received is excluded besides that which has been received up until now, is expressly taught in the Vatican Council: "If anyone shall assert it to be possible that sometimes, according to the progress of science, a sense is to be given to doctrines propounded by the Church different from that which the Church has understood and understands; let him be anathema."[210] Elsewhere this is taught more fully: "For the doctrine of faith, which God has revealed has not been proposed,

209 Wis. 6, 14 & 18.
210 Dz. 1818.

like a philosophical invention, to be perfected by human ingenuity. Rather, it has been delivered as a Divine deposit to the Spouse of Christ, to be faithfully kept and infallibly declared. Hence also, that meaning of the sacred dogmas is perpetually to be retained which our Holy Mother the Church has once declared. Nor is that meaning ever to be departed from, under the pretense or pretext of a deeper comprehension of them."[211]

More explicitly still by Pius X, the error which we here attack, concerning new truths of the faith being added to the deposit, is reproved by the following [condemned] propositions: "In the primitive Church the concept of the Christian sinner reconciled by the authority of the Church did not exist. Only very slowly did the Church accustom herself to this concept. As a matter of fact, even after Penance was recognized as an institution of the Church, it was not called a Sacrament since it would be held as a disgraceful Sacrament."[212]—"It is impossible that Matrimony could have become a Sacrament of the New Law until later in the Church since it was necessary that a full theological explication of the doctrine of grace and the Sacraments should first take place before Matrimony should be held as a Sacrament."[213]—"Christ did not teach a determined body of doctrine applicable to all times and all men, but rather inaugurated a religious movement adapted or to be adapted to different times and places."[214]

---

211 Dz. 1800.

212 *Lamentabili Sane*, prop. 46 (Dz. 2046).

213 *Ibid.*, prop. 51 (Dz. 2051).

214 *Ibid.*, prop. 59 (Dz. 2059). Cf. from this same Encyclical *Pascendi* in various places. G.Tyrell reduced this heap of errors into a synthesis as follows: "May not Catholicism, like Judaism, have to die in order that it may live again in a greater and grander form? Has not every organism its limits of development, after which it must decay and be content to survive in its progeny? Wine-skins

**18.—The error of those saying, that certain propositions are condemned because the time has not yet come for proclaiming them**—Which things being so, those who for this reason affirm that certain propositions are condemned by the Church because the time has not yet come for them to be openly proclaimed, ought to be said to have deviated far from the truth: who furthermore add that the authors of such propositions ought to submit themselves to those condemning those propositions, the ordered growth of things having required it, since in this way they can better conciliate the opinion of men towards themselves, and they ought to wait for a riper time, in which such teachings can be preached more opportunely and effectively. Certainly this practice, which we see widely adopted by the Modernists, truly supposes either that dogmas are changeable or new revelations are to be expected, besides what has until now been handed down: which two things are completely foreign to the Catholic truth.[215]

---

stretch, but only within measure; for there comes at last a bursting-point when new ones must be provided." (*Much-abused Letter* (London, Longmans, 1906), p. 89).

215 For this manner of acting, for the defense of which Fogazzaro has written the book, *Il Santo*, which was put on the Index of forbidden books, this sentence of Cardinal Newman (*Apologia*, p. 259) may perhaps give some occasion: "In reading ecclesiastical history, when I was an Anglican, it used to be forcibly brought home to me, how the initial error of what afterwards became heresy was the urging forward some truth against the prohibition of authority at an unseasonable time," etc. But even if it be by no means difficult to take this citation of Cardinal Newman in a good sense, still the things which are uttered in this sense by the Modernists are more serious than can allow a favorable interpretation. Hence very recently G. Tyrrell wrote as a mere calumny: "The solidity of Newmanism with Modernism cannot be denied. Newman might have shuddered at his progeny, but it is none the less his," etc. (*The Prospect of Modernism* in *The Hibbert Journal* (Jan. 1908, p. 243)).

# FIFTH QUESTION

## ON THE INCREASE OR PROGRESS OF SACRED DOCTRINE OR CATHOLIC DOGMA

### PROLOGUE

**1.—State of the Question**—Since sacred doctrine, or Catholic dogma, has the nature of a deposit entrusted to the guardianship of the Church, which is understood to have been sifted through the succession of time,[216] wherefore this momentous question is now proposed, namely, what kind of progress or evolution may be admitted in it.—It can scarcely be said how bitterly this matter, around which the whole hinge of Modernism turns, in these last times, has been disputed: for removing the doubt, not a few distinctions ought to be introduced, since nothing serves better to elucidate the truth than a clear division of things.

**2.—How many kinds of increase in science can be admitted**—Now it ought to be known that the increase in habits which connote an order to something knowable, for example it is precisely science which connotes an order to what is knowable, can be considered in two ways, as the Angelic Doctor says: in one way, in itself, as it is said, for example, greater science extends itself to many things, as it is also said that greater health which embraces more things in the human body; in another way, according to the participation of the subject; insofar as a truly equal knowledge according to the knowable objects, is nevertheless better received

---

216 "The knowledge of Divine things increased as time went on" (I, q. 57, a. 5 ad 3$^{um}$). Citation of St. Gregory the Great, *Homiliarum in Ezechielem*, lib. 2, hom. 4 (PL 76, 980B): "... *per incrementa temporum crevit scientia spiritualium patrum.*"

in one than in another according to men's different aptitudes, either from nature or from custom: in which way also greater health is said to be in one individual than in another, because although in both it extends itself to all parts of the body, still it is partaken of more intensely by one man than by another. In this way, therefore, when someone learns many conclusions of geometry, the habit of the same science is increased in him in regard to itself; but when it is had more readily and clearly in knowing and explaining the same conclusions, the geometric science is said to have increased according to the partaking of the subject, or according to intensity.

**3.—Note**—In which place we immediately point out that herein the terms "sacred doctrine" and "Catholic dogma" are used indiscriminately in various places: because, even if Catholic dogma strictly pertains to all the truths which the faithful, when put forth by the Church, are bound to hold, but sacred doctrine, as it was often said, abstracts from the notion of something known or believed, yet it also ultimately pertains to the deposit of faith, insofar as that if this be denied, it would be necessary that Catholic dogma suffers loss.

So that it will be easily established to anyone even cursorily perusing the outline, the question of the progress or evolution of sacred doctrine or Catholic dogma involves many problems in itself, to which it will be necessary that an answer be given, not one taken from the opinions of one or another writer, but one that reason itself will demonstrate, rightly drawn from the safest principles of theology.

**4.—Outline of the question**—But, on the other hand, so that the question about the growth, or progress of sacred doctrine or Catholic dogma may be fully discussed, it is necessary that it firstly be examined absolutely (1-6), and secondly, relatively, which is by comparison established between the knowledge of one man and the knowledge of another (7). Now the increase in the knowledge of sacred doctrine, absolutely considered, includes two questions: one, whether such increase may be given (1), secondly, how it may be effected (2-6). An increase of this kind can actually be effected by means both internal (2-5), and external (6). And the internal means are divided in two: for some are essential (2-4), others however are accidental, of which kind there are heresies, from which an occasion is given of shedding brighter light upon Catholic dogma (5). The means are again in a twofold distinction: namely, one is the supernatural means, which is the instinct of the Holy Ghost (2); but the other is natural (3-4), and in fact twofold: one is common to all, which is sacred scholastic doctrine (3); the other belongs to each of the faithful, namely his own exertion, or personal study (4).

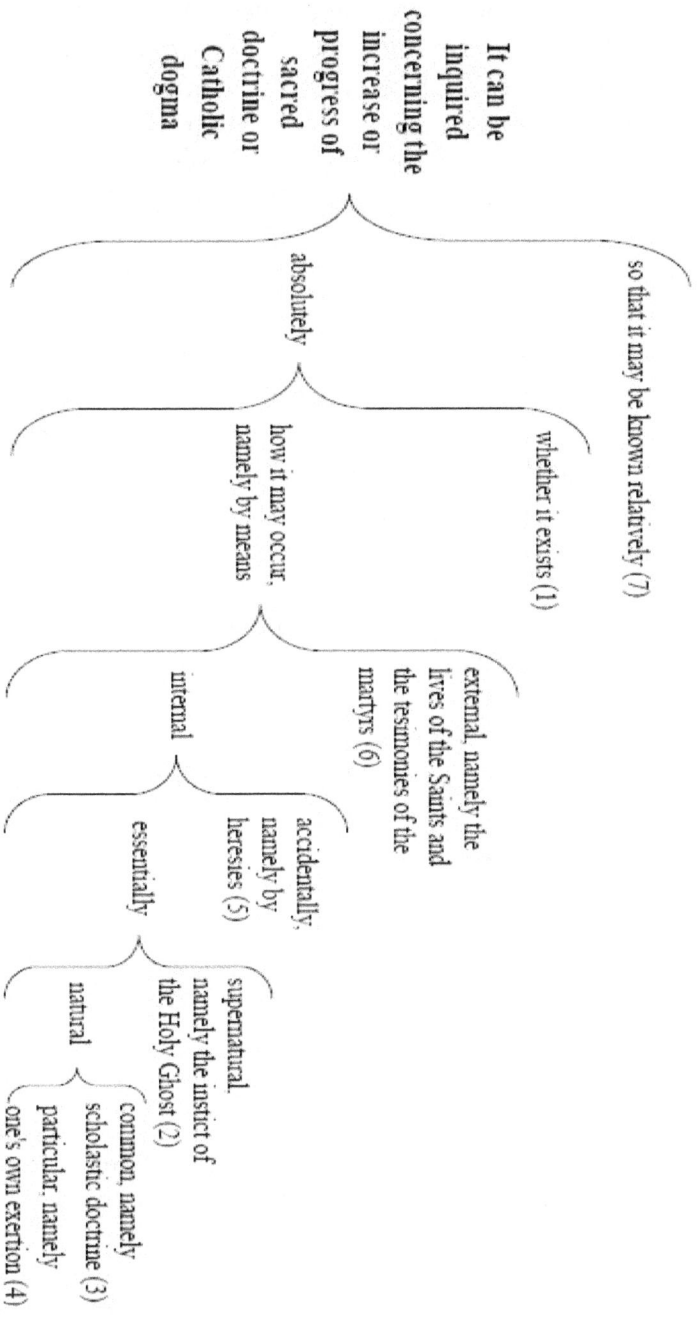

It can be inquired concerning the increase or progress of sacred doctrine or Catholic dogma

- so that it may be known relatively (7)
- absolutely
  - whether it exists (1)
  - how it may occur, namely by means
    - external, namely the lives of the Saints and the testimonies of the martyrs (6)
    - internal
      - accidentally, namely by heresies (5)
      - essentially
        - supernatural, namely the instinct of the Holy Ghost (2)
        - natural
          - common, namely scholastic doctrine (3)
          - particular, namely one's own exertion (4)

Hence seven points will be treated in this question.

*First.* Whether an increase in the manifestation of sacred doctrine can be given in the Church.

*Second.* Whether the faithful, by the instinct of the Holy Ghost, may believe and retain those things which were previously only implicitly held in the Church.

*Third.* Whether progress in the knowledge of the dogmas of the faith was done by an evolution of sacred scholastic doctrine.

*Fourth.* Whether by their own exertion and effort the individual faithful can advance in the knowledge of accepted dogmas.

*Fifth.* Whether by heresies springing up Catholic dogma has been better elucidated.

*Sixth.* Whether by the lives of the Saints and testimonies of the martyrs, Catholic dogma was clarified.

*Seventh.* Whether the knowledge of the dogmas of the Catholic faith can be greater in one man than in another.

**ARTICLE 1—*Whether an increase in the manifestation of sacred doctrine can be given in the Church.***

**1.—State of the question**—Since we have shown how both Divine revelation and the definitions of the Church ought to be accepted, it is now easy for us to investigate whether and how the development in the manifestation of dogma over the course of time, keeping its immutability, could take place: which in fact will be determined here by a more general notion, leaving the more particular exposition of the same matter to the subsequent articles, both in regard to the universal Church, and relatively to its individual members.

We have already said,[217] that a twofold increase in sciences, absolutely speaking, can be considered; one,

---

217 See n. 2 above.

on the part of the science considered in itself; the other, according to the participation of the subject. Thus since the possibility of an increase in revelation according to itself ought to be excluded, not in fact from God's absolute power, but from God's ordained power, it now spontaneously follows that it may be clearly determined whether and how an increase can be admitted as to a clearer knowledge, a richer illustration and a more useful exposition of the same revelation may be had in the Church.

**2.—Explicit and implicit knowledge**—Next, a further distinction ought to be considered between that which is explicitly known, and that which can be only held implicitly: certainly, it can indeed happen that someone previously retaining the whole deposit of the faith implicitly, afterwards nevertheless believes each point contained in it more explicitly; certainly not such that he believes a new dogma, but such that he may newly hold it, meaning in a new and more explicit way.—Which things being so, the question ought to be understood of such increase in the manifestation of the dogma, whereby something may be afterwards believed explicitly, which previously was held only implicitly and as in the root.

**3.—Proposition I—An increase ought to be admitted in the manifestation of Catholic dogma.**

**4.—Explanation**—Of course, anyone who has briefly considered the words of the Christ the Lord to the Apostles, or who has very generally applied his mind to that law whereby all things which are in the world, either natural or supernatural, are governed, could scarcely doubt that some development, or fuller and more explicit preaching and manifestation of dogma, with the passing of centuries, ought to be had.

And in fact, which belongs to the first place, when Our Lord was saying: "But the Paraclete, the Holy Ghost, whom the Father will send in my name, he will teach you all things, and bring all things to your mind, whatsoever I shall have said to you,"[218]—what else did He mean, except that His Apostles and their successors, as well as the whole multitude of the faithful, or the Church, will advance in the dogma received for the instruction of the faith and the purity of morals?

But also since the process of the supernatural order in some way corresponds to the course of the natural order, the law however in this order being constant, assuredly it is that imperfect things, and this only gradually, attain to their more complete development, and what remains but that a more full and complete manifestation of the revelation, which is the form of the supernatural order, is to be expected, under the influence of the Holy Ghost, to be completed with the passing of time?

In this way therefore we now see many things are held more explicitly and more overtly, which previously were believed just implicitly and somewhat obscurely, as for example there are many things which pertain to the economy of the Sacraments, to the veneration of the Saints, and generally to the spiritual life of the Church.—Here the golden words of Blessed Albert the Great ought to be noted, where he says that growth of this kind is "of the faithful in the faith, rather than of faith in the faithful."[219]

**5.—Comparison of the natural and super- natural order**—Here, however, one must be carefully on his guard lest the established comparison between the natural order and the supernatural order be so

---

218 Jn. 14, 26.

219 *Super IV libros Sententiarum* (ed. Borgnet, 1893-4), lib. III, dist. XXV, art. 1, ad 1$^{\text{um}}$.

drawn out that the growth we see in natural sciences be expected to be proportionally realized in the theological discipline, since one is the notion of the natural sciences, and another is that of sacred doctrine. For the former by the strength of natural intelligence, as to its own and proportionate agent, is cultivated; the latter, however, since it is the expression of God's science, and is supported by the faith, which is God's gift, has God for its principal author, to Whom accordingly it pertains, as to the proper agent, to establish the appropriate times for greater and more ample development of doctrine, assuredly to be completed by men, as by instruments.

Therefore, if some opinion prevails at some time in the Christian people, and it has its origin from God, there is no doubt that, notwithstanding any contradiction, its knowledge with the passing of time would so develop, that finally the Church's either explicit or implicit sanction would come to it. But if, on the contrary, such an opinion has a human origin, it will quickly be obscured, until at last it either falls into oblivion, or it is censured by the Church. An example of this can be the opinion of the Immaculate Conception both of the Blessed Virgin and of St. Joseph, her spouse, which twofold opinion we know was in favor at one time during the Middle Ages. But, with the passing of time, the prior opinion, as inspired by God, received an continual increase in the minds of the faithful, until at last it was infallibly defined by the Church; but the other opinion, as having arisen from men, has now clearly fallen into oblivion.

**6.—How an increase may occur in the knowledge of revelation**—It is also necessary to beware of something else, namely lest the progress in the manifestation and knowledge of revelation, or of sacred doctrine, be said to happen by means of natural disciplines: for granted that these also have some order to revelation, since there is but one end of man and the role of nature is to subserve grace, still the natural sciences alone left to themselves are unequal to the task to even in the least way increase knowledge of the supernatural order; hence we also see many very famous cultivators of the natural sciences certainly very far from the faith, but on the contrary, more uneducated and simpler men giving compliance to things of the faith with the whole affection of their hearts and minds: which is the case, not because natural sciences of themselves turn men away from the faith, but rather because sometimes that promptitude and self-effacement of soul is lacking in man, which is a necessary condition for embracing the faith. But if, along with self-effacement of soul, a fuller knowledge of scientific things be had, yet as long as it be genuine and not spurious, full and not superficial, then, with the Lord helping, this knowledge can be very useful for the building up of the faith.

7.—**How knowledge of Catholic dogma may increase**—Now in this way knowledge of Catholic dogma slowly increases, such that a later age receives more explicit knowledge from that which previously was retained only implicitly. Then this addition of knowledge, however minuscule it may be, if the centuries immediately succeeding each other are considered, with the passing of time, it certainly appears great, to such an extent that if someone would compare the faith of previous centuries to the faith of our time, without any regard to the centuries which intervened, he will easily begin to suspect what was believed in ancient times is not substantially the same thing that is held now. Thus if someone would wish to correctly trace the history of the dogmas of the faith, he ought not to otherwise proceed than as one who desires to investigate the first source of a splendid river: certainly, he ought to go up higher, follow the current up until he arrives at the originating spring; for if he would directly compare the spring with the river, he will not be able to certainly detect the identity of one with the other. Or again if someone has only two pictures of a certain man before his eyes, one when he was in his early youth, the other when he is represented in extreme old age, it will indeed hardly suffice to identify the man, whose pictures they are; but if one has many pictures, he will detect him to be the same man without difficulty, although he has a different age, to whom now hoary old wrinkled faces grow pale, and who long before was flourishing in the flower of age as first quinces bestrewn with their first down.

**8.—Whether Catholic dogma can be called a seed**—It will help here to repeat the epitome of equivocation, whence many were deceived to such a degree, that they presumed to introduce some change in the very substance of Catholic dogma. Namely those who seemed supported by the parable in which Our Lord says that the kingdom of heaven is "like to a grain of mustard seed, which a man took and sowed in his field. Which is the least indeed of all seeds; but when it is grown up, it is greater than all herbs, and becometh a tree, so that the birds of the air come, and dwell in the branches thereof."[220] Therefore, since Divine revelation is not unsuitably compared to a seed, then some well-known authors assert that the progress of evolution in Catholic dogma is realized similarly to the progress which we see accomplished every day in worldly affairs.

**9.—The evolution of dogma according to Cardinal Newman**—In which matter, it helps to reflect upon the way by which the celebrated writer, Cardinal Newman, attempts to explain this progress. Namely, from the analogy and example of Scripture, he says,

---

220 Mt. 13, 31-32.

formal, legitimate and true development can be admitted in Christian doctrine, and they have been ordained by its Divine Author.[221] And the same author continues unfolding his mind with comparisons brought forth from the celebrated Anglican writer, Butler,[222] from the succession and change of the seasons of the year, from the production of flowers, the maturation of fruits and also the development of the life of animals and men.[223] From all which things he concludes that a similar progress is had in Christian doctrine, insofar as the vital seed of revelation gradually was developed from a more imperfect to a more perfect state, through the absorption of food from without, which at length was assimilated through its nutritive power, and converted into its substance.[224]

**10.—Notice**—About which, in the first place, we notice that the initial tradition of Catholic dogma, which in fact we can call only in an broad sense a living thing, compared to the more perfect and abundant manifestation of the same dogma, not being completely related as a seed compared to tree or to an animal: for a seed is

---

221 "From the analogy and example of Scripture, we may fairly conclude that Christian doctrine admits of formal, legitimate and true developments contemplated by its Divine Author." (*An Essay on the Development*, etc., p. 74)

222 *Analogy*, II, 4, at the end.

223 "The change of seasons, the ripening of the earth, the very history of a flower is an instance of this; and so is human life. Thus vegetable bodies, and those of animals, though possibly formed at once, yet grow up by degrees to a mature state. (Work cited, p. 74)

224 "In the physical world, whatever has life is characterized by growth, so that in no respect to grow is to cease to live. It grows by taking into its own substance external materials and this absorption or assimilation is completed when the materials appropriated come to belong to it or enter into its unity... This analogy may be taken to illustrate certain peculiarities in the growth or development in ideas, which were noticed in the first Chapter." (work cited, pp. 185-186)

not actually a small tree or a small animal, but it is a tree or animal in potency; and so only by a substantial change does a seed actually become a tree or animal: on the contrary, no substantial change in dogma can be admitted. Much less can it be admitted that the deposit of revelation grew from the additions coming from without and transmuted into the substance of that revelation: this position, in fact, which many recent authors have been forbidden to hold, is the source or origin of very serious errors: wherefore this error on this subject ought to be rejected in the praised Cardinal.

**11.—Catholic dogma can be rightly compared with leaven**—Thus by this comparison, being inadequate, nay being most dangerous, having been put aside, another more suitable comparison of Catholic dogma is made with "leaven, which a woman took and hid in three measures of meal, until the whole was leavened"[225]: for as the word "leaven" [*fermentum*], is taken from the word "boiling" [*fervendo*], as though "the cause of heating" [*fervi mentum*] were said, because it heats, raises, and inflates the mass kneaded for bread making, into which it is cast, so the sacred deposit of revelation, cast into the hearts of men, heats them, as though from fire set beneath, and as by holy heat, it stirs up one for any good deeds to be done and for suitable conclusions of doctrine.[226]

Still, a certain intrinsic fermentative power is also put into a seed: hence on this account Catholic dogma could be called a seed, which when planted sprouts in the hearts of men and breaks forth into the good fruits

---

225 Mt. 13, 33.

226 Cardinal Newman has recourse to this figure of speech when he writes: "Again the Parable of Leaven describes the development of doctrine in another respect, in its active, engrossing and interpenetrating power." (Work cited, p. 74).

of doctrine and piety when ripened with time: and actually in this sense the saying of Our Lord will be understood: "The seed is the word of God."[227]

**12.—The development of dogma explained by the comparison of a child to an adult or of the sapling to a tree**—Therefore having rejected the comparison of the seed related to a tree with the deposit of revelation related to successive developments, since a seed does not develop into a tree except by a substantial change of the thing, whereas in no dogma may such a change be given, it follows that we inquire whether it can be said that the initial revelation can be related to its later explanation, as a child to an adult, or as we see a sapling related to a lofty and verdant tree.

To which we reply that this comparison is very fitting, and completely suited for illustrating our matter, but it should be kept within due limits: namely, the comparison is upheld in this, that a lofty tree is indeed is as a species and individually the same plant as a sapling, but more elucidated and more actualized as to all its parts, and likewise an adult is as human as a child, but more perfect and stronger; the comparison fails, however, whenever it be considered in relation to the external nourishment which the sapling or child needs to grow to full size.

**13.—The preceding teaching explained**—Indeed in reality, the comparison taken to this extent, fails on this account, namely that it is found to have been explicitly condemned in this proposition of the decree *Lamentabili*: "Dogmas, Sacraments and hierarchy, both their notion and reality, are only interpretations and evolutions of the Christian intelligence which have in-

---

227 Lk. 8, 11.

creased and perfected by an external series of additions the little germ latent in the Gospel."[228]

On the contrary, to what extent the aforesaid comparison is verified is excellently explained by St. Vincent of Lérins. "But someone will say, perhaps, 'Shall there, then, be no progress in Christ's Church?' Certainly; all possible progress. For what being is there, so envious of men, so full of hatred toward God, who would seek to forbid it? Yet on condition that it be real progress, not alteration of the faith. For progress requires that the subject be enlarged in itself, alteration, that it be transformed into something else... The growth of religion in the soul must be analogous to the growth of the body, which, though in process of years it is developed and attains its full size, yet remains still the same. There is a wide difference between the flower of youth and the maturity of age; yet they who were once young are still the same now that they have become old, insomuch that though the stature and outward form of the individual are changed, yet his nature is one and the same, his person is one and the same. An infant's limbs are small, a young man's large, yet the infant and the young man are the same. Men when full grown have the same number of limbs that they had when children... In like

----

228 Prop. 54 (Dz. 2054). The very bad teaching summarized by this proposition is found in two works of Loisy: *L'Evangile et l'Eglise* and *Autour d'un petit livre*. According to this innovator, from the seed hidden in the Gospel and developed by the doctrinal authority of the Church, the reason for substantial difference between to-day's dogma and the dogma of the early Church should be derived; to such an extent that it ought to be said: "Le catholicisme consiste à recevoir, comme émanant d'une autorité divinement établie, l'interprétation que l'Église donne actuellement de l'Évangile" ["Catholicism consists in embracing, as emanating from a divinely established authority, the Church's present interpretation of the Gospel"]. (*Autour d'un petit livre*, p. 205).

manner, it behooves Christian doctrine to follow the same laws of progress, so as to be consolidated by years, enlarged by time, refined by age, and yet, withal, to continue incorrupt and unadulterated... For it is right that those ancient doctrines of heavenly philosophy should, as time goes on, be cared for, smoothed, polished; but not that they should be changed, not that they should be maimed, not that they should be mutilated. They may receive proof, illustration, definiteness; but they must retain withal their completeness, their integrity, their characteristic properties."[229]

**14.—Nothing foreign can be added to the deposit of revelation**—Therefore, granted that the early preaching of dogma is related to its later knowledge as a child to a man, in the sense that the man is the same person who was a child, only more developed in form, the comparison ought to be diligently rejected whenever the development is asserted to happen through nutrition, or by conversion of extrinsic consumed nourishment into the substance, namely insofar as that matter coming from outside truly receives the species of the plant or animal. It is indeed impossible that something extrinsic be joined or added to the deposit of revelation, without its nature being changed: for it belongs to the nature of revelation that it be derived from God, but those extrinsic additions are something human and so are of a lower nature.

But if one would like a more suitable example of the development or progress of Catholic dogma to be found, we will say that this is furnished by grace, which in heaven is glory, not by the addition of something extrinsic, but by its very consummation, under the action of the Holy Ghost.

---

229 *Commonitory*, c. 23, n. 54-56 (PL 50, 667-669).

**15.—The evolution of Catholic dogma according to the Modernists**—These things being so, it entirely belongs to the Modernistic contagion that it be said that Christian revelation was enriched by extrinsic additions: which can be feigned in two ways, namely either such that later persons—for example, John—relative to those Gospels they call the synoptics,[230] did not present anything but merely added from hagiographers to the doctrine of the preceding writers according to the current opinions of his time and place; or such that Catholic dogma by the very interaction of the Church with civil society, through the course of centuries, gradually acquired various elements borrowed from it, until it obtained the present form, actually quite dissonant from the antique form, yet desired by the very condition of the dogma. And this is precisely that development which Pius X condemned by these words: "Christian Doctrine was originally Judaic. Through successive evolutions it became first Pauline, then Joannine, finally Hellenic and universal."[231]

**16.—The comparison of dogma to a seed**—Next, since the comparison between the deposit of revelation and a seed, in relation to the subsequent development of both, cannot be upheld entirely, still nothing prevents us from applying the parable of the grain of mustard seed to our matter in some way, namely by understanding by the grain of this kind not in fact the revelation itself, but the preaching of Catholic dogma, namely both active preaching, which is accomplished by the oral teaching of the pastors, and passive preaching, which consists in the wider knowledge and acceptance of the announced doctrine.

---

230 See what we have said in *Diatesseron*, vol. I, Introd., n. XXVII, p. XXXVII.

231 Prop. 60 in the decree, *Lamentabili* (Dz 2060).

**17.—St. Jerome on the development of Christian preaching**—And this is indeed what St. Jerome very eloquently explains, when commenting on the cited parable of the grain of mustard seed: "Who is it that sows except the mind and heart, which upon receiving the grain of preaching and nurturing the seed sown with the moisture of faith causes it to sprout in the field of his heart? The preaching of the Gospel is the least of all instruction. Indeed, in the initial teaching, it does not have the conviction of truth. It preaches a God Who is a man, a Christ Who died, and the scandal of the Cross. Compare the doctrine of this sort with the doctrines of the philosophers, with their books, and with the splendor of their eloquence and the composition of their words. Then you will see how much the sowing of the Gospel is less than the other seeds. But when those seeds grow, they demonstrate no bite, no vigor, not vitality. They are entirely flaccid and droopy. They sprout forth into garden plants and herbs which quickly wither and fall. But this preaching, which seemed trivial at the beginning, when it has been sown, either into the soul of the believer or into the whole world, does not rise up into a garden plant, but it grows into a tree, so that the birds of the sky, which we ought to understand as the souls of believers or their resolutions submitted to the service of God, come and dwell in its branches. I think the branches of the Gospel-tree which grows from the grain of mustard seed are the diverse kinds of dogmas in which each of the above-mentioned birds finds rest."[232]

It ought not to disturb the reader that St. Jerome here calls the various dogmas "branches of the Gospel-tree," namely as though from that seed from the first period, the dogmas at a later time sprouted: in fact, according to the provided metaphor, the Gospel-tree is the same

---

232 *Commentary on Matthew*, bk. 2, c. 13, v. 32 (PL 26, 90B-C).

preaching of the Gospel, which certainly obtained increase, with which the explicit faith of the Christian people also grew, as we shall say below.[233]

**18.—The Creed**—Now to this which we say here, namely the increase or progress in the manifestation of Catholic dogma is given in the Church by Divine institution, properly pertains a new version of the Creed, concerning which matter, on account of the article *Filioque* added long ago to the Nicene-Constantinopolitan Creed was long discussed in the Council of Florence.[234] Doubtlessly, as against Bessarion asserting that absolutely any insertion made into the Creed ought to be rejected as an addition, John, bishop of Forli-Bertinoro, eloquently remarked,[235] that if the great multitude of mysteries of the New Testament, which are implicitly contained in the Old Covenant, cannot be properly called an addition, in respect to the meaning, it ought not to be surprising if the explanations of those mysteries which are now given, ought not to be deemed additions, but only as new explanations of those things which of their nature are obscure.[236]

Quite a long time ago the Angelic Doctor, with his usual perspicacity of mind, wrote about this matter as follows: "This prohibition and sentence of the council [of Ephesus decreeing that no one is allowed bring forth, profess, or compose another faith besides what was defined by the holy Fathers, who were gathered together with the Holy Ghost in Nicea] was intended for private individuals, who have no business to decide matters of

---

233 We have mentioned above the excellent comparison of the development of dogma with the deduction of conclusions from the premises.

234 See the *Acta Conc. Florent.*, Labbe, Concil., vol. 13, pp. 130 ff.

235 Sess. X Conc. Ferrar.

236 Labbe, *op. cit.*, p. 154.

faith: for this decision of the general council did not take away from a subsequent council the power of drawing up a new version of the Creed, containing not indeed a new faith, but the same faith with greater explicitness. For every council has taken into account that a subsequent council would expound matters more fully than the preceding council, if this became necessary through some heresy arising. Consequently this belongs to the Sovereign Pontiff, by whose authority the council is convoked, and its decision confirmed."[237]

**19.—The Catholic Church is not impervious to progress**—From the things deduced in this article, it can be by no means inferred what the chattering critics of the Church babble, namely that theology precludes the increase of scientific progress, or it is itself a retrograde discipline. For Sacred doctrine does not fear, but seeks the light, and fosters the growth of all sciences, by which it is rendered illustrious in more and more marvelous ways. But also while keeping the firmness of its principles it admits progress in its explanation and proof; for, although revelation ended with the death of the Apostles, hence it is not subject to progress as being an increase, still with the Divine assistance, it admits a continual advancement in its exposition.

Wherefore one nowise ought to assent to that which Macaulay propounds, who is of the opinion that the notion of the Catholic Church's indefectibility is to be derived from the fact that theological science is not subject to progress; natural theology, he says, is not subject to progress, which from the same effects, from which we now perceive God's existence, could know the same thing at the beginning; theology, which draws from revelation, is not subject to progress, because all revelation is contained in Scripture, to which not even a word can be

237 II-II, q. 1, a. 10 ad 2[um].

added, be there whatsoever attempts: such that, having supposed the same good faith and the same natural sagacity, a Christian of the nineteenth century, who has Scripture, is completely on a par with a Christian of the fifth century equally having Scripture; hence, he concludes, men will never return to the system of Ptolemy, given the progress in the natural sciences; but, by no development having transpired in the Catholic religion, men go backwards in time to transubstantiation.[238]

Certainly, even if it were true that there never had been any progress at all in the Catholic Church, either regarding definitions, such as are had in the Councils, or regarding the exposition of doctrine, such as afforded by the scholastic theology, or in liturgical rites, or in the canons of discipline, the very fact that the above-mentioned Church has both so strenuously withstood and invincibly crushed various and repeated aggressions against the dogma and truths proclaimed by it, is more brilliant and outstanding than all progress of the physical disciplines.

**20.—Difficulty solved**—Against the progress of this kind in the faith it could be objected that nature also takes

---

238 The diligent reader may distinguish for himself the truth from the falsity in the following words of this author: "All Divine truth is, according to the Protestant churches, recorded in certain books: it is equally open to all who, in any way, can read those books... A Christian of the fifth century with a Bible is on a par with a Christian of the nineteenth century with a Bible, candor and natural acuteness being, of course, supposed equal... We are confident that the world will never go back to the solar system of Ptolemy..., but we are very differently affected when we reflect that Sir Thomas More was ready to die for the doctrine of transubstantiation... We are, therefore, unable to understand why what Sir Thomas More believed respecting transubstantiation may not be believed to the end of time by men equal in abilities and honesty to Sir Thomas More." (*Rank's History of the Popes*. Essay. London, 1889, p. 573-574).

its beginning from perfect things; but now the operation of grace does not proceed less orderly than the operation of nature; thus it seems that those who firstly handed down the faith, knew it most perfectly, and so progress in the knowledge of the faith cannot be admitted.[239]

To which it can replied with the Angelic Doctor,[240] in the order of nature, two causes preexist for natural generation: namely, the efficient cause and the material cause. Therefore, regarding the order of the efficient cause, that which is more perfect is naturally first, and thus nature takes its beginning from perfect things: for imperfect things are not brought to perfection except from some preexisting perfect things. Now regarding the order of the material cause, that which is more imperfect is prior, and according to this nature proceeds from the imperfect to the perfect. Thus, in the generation of man. regarding the order of the efficient cause, the perfect things precede the imperfect thing, since man is not generated except from a grown man; but regarding the order of the material cause, it is the reverse, since a child is prior to a man.

Therefore, in the order of grace, in those things which pertain to the manifestation of the faith, God is like an agent, Who has perfect wisdom from eternity, but man is like the matter receiving the influx of God the Agent; and thus it was necessary that the knowledge of the faith in men would proceed from imperfect things to the perfect.

**21.—Proposition II—The aforesaid increase formally pertains to the Church learning.**

**22.—Explanation**—In order that how the above-mentioned increase of knowledge in the Church has a place may be understood, one ought to carefully consider the

---

239 So says St. Thomas in obj. 3.
240 *Ibid.*

difference which is between human science and the sacred doctrine of the faith.

Certainly, in sciences humanly attained through reason, the advancement of knowledge pertains to the one teaching, who advances in knowledge, whether he be one or many through the succession of time, and this is due the defect of knowledge in the first men who established the sciences, as Aristotle maintains;[241] but, in the doctrine of the faith, which is not humanly established, but Divinely handed down, for it is God's gift, the increase formally belongs to the learners, to whom God gives more abundant knowledge with the passage of time. Indeed, just as a teacher who knew the whole art, yet does not immediately at the beginning pass it on to his disciple, who would be unable to grasp it, but condescending slowly does so according to his capacity, so God did not hand down immediately at the beginning the whole knowledge of supernatural things, but little by little, so that men might advance in the knowledge of the faith through the passage of time: wherefore the Apostle compares the state of the Old Testament to childhood, when he says: "Wherefore the law was our pedagogue in Christ."[242]

Which things being so, those investigators of sacred things ought to be greatly reprehended, who so seek the notion of evolution of dogmas or of Catholic worship as though the very Church teaching itself, groping in the dark with its hands, slowly accommodated the received teaching of Christ to the people's moral abilities and intellectual culture among whom it lived, and in this manner it at last composed its Creed, as though finally discovered, coming forth from the collaboration of many men. Certainly, it follows that the most perfect

241 *Metaphyic.*, bk. 2, text 1 & 2.
242 Gal. 3, 24.

possession of all supernatural truths already belonged to the Church teaching from its first beginning, which nevertheless it had to explain to the people entrusted to it not otherwise than according to the diversity of times and persons.

**23.—The diversity of progress in the doctrine of the faith to be handed down in regard to the Church teaching**—Next, when we mention the Church teaching, if we would in fact wish to speak concretely, assuredly it firstly and especially consists of Christ the Lord, Who is the invisible Head of the Church, and secondarily of the legitimate teachers, who are the popes, bishops, Fathers and Doctors. Indeed, in that it pertains to Christ, it is evident that He had the fullness of knowledge; and when He promised to be with the Church all days even to the consummation of the world, we then have full confidence that the full knowledge about matters of faith will never be lacking in the Church.

Now regarding men who are teachers of the faith, two things ought to be carefully considered.

Firstly, it ought to be noted in general that the final consummation of grace was made by Christ, wherefore also His time is called the "fulness of time,"[243] hence those who lived nearer to Christ, either before, such as John the Baptist, or afterwards, such as the Apostles, knew the mysteries of faith more fully; for likewise concerning the natural state of man, we see that his perfection is in youth, and a man has so much more perfect state, either before or after, the more he is closer to being young. Hence likewise the interlinear Gloss on the passage: "We ourselves who have the firstfruits of the Spirit,"[244] says that the Apostles received "as being

---

243 Gal. 4, 4.
244 Rom. 8, 23.

first in time, so also more abundantly than others,"[245] hence also we read it said prophetically about them: "The eyes of them that see shall not be dim, and the ears of them that hear shall hearken diligently. And the heart of fools shall understand knowledge, and the tongue of stammerers shall speak readily and plain."[246]

Now because we are speaking about the knowledge of Divine things, it also ought to be said concerning hope, in regard to the obtaining the things promised: without doubt, as the Angelic Doctor likewise argues: "Among men the same things were always to be hoped for from Christ. But as they did not acquire this hope save through Christ, the further they were removed from Christ in point of time, the further they were from obtaining what they hoped for. Hence the Apostle says: 'All these died according to faith, not having received the promises, but beholding them afar off.'[247] Now the further off a thing is the less distinctly is it seen; wherefore those who were nigh to Christ's advent had a more distinct knowledge of the good things to be hoped for."[248]

From which things, as Cajetan suitably remarks, it follows of itself that "in the determination of questions of faith, the teaching of the Doctors and of the holy Fathers is to be taken, *whom we believe to have been enlightened with Divine light both as to teaching and as to life rather than of those who lived later, whenever later men differ from them.*"[249]

---

245 Gloss, ad 4^m.

246 Is. 32, 3-4.

247 Heb. 11, 13.

248 Ibid., ad 1^um.

249 *Commentarius in Summam Th,*, II-II, q. 1, a. 7. [*Translator's note*: John of St. Thomas likewise wrote: "Otherwise I think what the Apostles knew through infused knowledge, the truths which theologians have now obtained through discursive reasoning, pertaining to the mysteries of the faith; and I speak about truths and

Nevertheless, what Cajetan likewise advises afterwards ought not to be overlooked, namely that it can happen that, "even after Christ, *a later century may have more outstanding Doctors in these things which belong to the faith than some previous century, although not more than every century, for instance, in the era of the year one thousand there were more learned doctors in the faith than in the era of the year eight hundred; because even if Divine doctrine regularly proceeds according to the nearness to Christ, still its illumination is not bound to this order. A sign of which is that Moses is believed to have been elevated to the vision of the Divine essence, to which no one afterwards and nearer to Christ is believed to have been elevated. Still there never were or will be more learned men than the Apostles, just as there will also not be more perfect men."*[250]

The other thing that ought to be noted is that the men whom God used as instruments for spreading the knowledge of the faith enjoyed fuller knowledge so far as the manifestation of His Spirit was given for the common good, as St. Paul intimates;[251] [as St Thomas said:] "so that the knowledge of faith was imparted to the Fathers who were instructors in the faith, so far as was necessary at the time for the instruction of the people, either openly

---

not opinions, which are subject to being false. Similarly I am persuaded that the holy Fathers, from whose writings the scholastics take their teaching, knew the truths which the theologians receive from them through discursive reasoning, and although they did not have such full infused knowledge as the Apostles, still I would suppose that they wrote many things by a special instinct of the Holy Ghost, which pertain to morals and the doctrine of the faith." (*Cursus theologicus*, q. 1 de fide, disputatio 6, a. 2, n. 20).]

250 *Ibid.*

251 "And the manifestation of the Spirit is given to every man unto profit" (I Cor. 12, 7).

or in figures,"[252] hence the progress of the Doctors redounds unto the benefit of those being instructed.

**24.—In regard to acquired knowledge, the knowledge of matters of faith grows together with the passing of time**—Nevertheless, here we ought to further distinguish the knowledge of matters of our faith imparted or infused by God, from acquired knowledge; and in fact, those things which were said until now concerning the fuller knowledge according to the greater nearness to Christ, ought to be understood of Divinely infused knowledge, or imparted by revelation: still that knowledge once communicated to God's people was transmitted to later generations, so that they might receive it and deduce fitting conclusions from the principles shown; whence it is said: "Ask thy father, and he will declare to thee: thy elders and they will tell thee."[253] Wherefore, if indeed acquired science be regarded, it should be said that the knowledge of matters of faith grows with the passing of time, such that it becomes fuller, the more the centuries are multiplied: which St. Gregory the Great explains as follows: "The more the world is brought to its end, so much the more is the access to eternal knowledge opened more broadly."[254]

**25.—Question I**—*What progress was made in the handing down of revelation with the passing of time up until the Apostles?*

*Reply.* Since our faith especially consists in two things, namely, *first*, in the true knowledge of the one and triune God, and *second*, in the sincere recognition of Christ's Incarnation, which are the two principal mysteries of our faith, in order that it may be known

---

252 II-II, q. 1, a. 7 ad 3$^{um}$.

253 Deut. 32, 7.

254 Homily 16 on the Gospels, vol. 2, p. 230; *Expositio Veteris ac Novi Testamenti*, bk. 6, c. 10 (PL 79, 1002D).

what progress occurred with the passing of time in the manifestation or handing down of revelation up until the Apostles, it is necessary to investigate how the deposit of revelation grew, in both respects, according to the diversities of the times.

And firstly, in fact, regarding faith in the true God, three different times can be assigned: namely before the Law, under the Law and after the Law, or under grace.

Before the Law, we see Abraham and the other Patriarchs Divinely instructed concerning those things which pertain to faith in the Deity, or concerning monotheism: now because this knowledge was granted to them by prophetic light, it follows that those men, especially Abraham and Isaac, are called prophets, according to the passage: "Do no evil to my prophets."[255]—Under the Law, however, the manifestation of the Deity, namely about those things which pertain to faith in the Deity,[256] is found to be done more excellently than before, both according to the extension and according to the perfection of the revelation: according to the extension, for not only specific persons or families were Divinely instructed about monotheism, but the whole nation; according to the perfection, for while the preceding Patriarchs were taught regarding faith in the omnipotence of the one God, Moses on the other hand was more fully instructed about the simplicity of the Divine essence, since it was explicitly said to him: "I am Who am,"[257] because it was customary for the Jews to signify the tetragrammaton name by substituting in its place the name, *Adonai*, on account of the highest veneration for that ineffable name: hence we read: "I am the Lord, that ap-

---

255 Ps. 104, 15.

256 Here it is said: "which pertain to faith in the Deity": for, what pertains to the government of life, will be said below, n. 25.

257 Ex. 3, 14.

peared to Abraham, to Isaac, and to Jacob, by the name of God Almighty; and my name Adonai I did not shew them."[258]—Finally in the time of grace, the mystery of the Trinity was explicitly revealed by the Son of God Himself, according to the passage: "Going therefore, teach ye all nations; baptizing them in the name of the Father, and of the Son, and of the Holy Ghost."[259]

Now it ought to be observed that in each of these three states, the faith of the those coming afterwards was founded upon the revelation made to those who were the heads or foundations of those states: thus the faith of Isaac and Jacob was founded upon the revelation made to Abraham, when God said to Isaac: "I am the God of Abraham thy father,"[260] and to Jacob: "I am the Lord God of Abraham thy father, and the God of Isaac."[261]— Similarly the faith of the whole Hebraic nation was founded upon the revelation made to Moses.—Lastly, in the time of grace, the whole faith of the Church was founded upon the revelation made to the Apostles concerning the faith of the unity and trinity, according to the passage: "Upon this rock," namely of your confession, O Peter, "I will build my Church."[262]

Secondly, regarding faith in the Incarnation, it is evident that the more men were closer to Christ, either before or after the Incarnation, that ordinarily, the more they were instructed about this mystery; hence St. Gregory the Great, when speaking about the Incarnation, says that "knowledge of God went on increasing as time went on";[263] although it ought to be said that the knowledge of

---

258 Ex. 6, 2-3.
259 Mt. 28, 19.
260 Gen. 26, 24.
261 Gen. 28, 13.
262 Mt. 16, 18.
263 *In Ezech.*, bk. 2, homily 16 cited according to the meaning; *Homiliarum in Ezechielem*, lib. 2, hom. 4 (PL 76, 980B): "... *per in-*

this mystery was by far more abundant after the Incarnation than before, according to the passage of St. Paul: "As you reading, may understand my knowledge in the mystery of Christ, which in other generations was not known to the sons of men, as it is now revealed to his holy Apostles and prophets in the Spirit."[264]

Notice therefore how was, with the passing of time, delineated by the main points, the development of the manifestation or tradition of the revelation, which in fact unto Adam, immediately after the fall, we see having begun, increased in the Patriarchs and Moses, and perfected in the Apostles, by the Holy Ghost Himself showing them the Divine mysteries and thus completing the instruction of the Incarnate Word, according to the promise of Christ the Lord Himself: "But the Paraclete, the Holy Ghost, whom the Father will send in my name, he will teach you all things, and bring all things to your mind, whatsoever I shall have said to you."[265]

**26.—Question II—** *By what kind of norm or law was this development or progress of the manifestation of revelation done?*

*Reply.* There is no other norm of the knowledge of the truths which pertain to this order besides necessity, for leading men to eternal life; hence we see that the revelation of monotheism was made just only at the time of Abraham, at which time men began to deviate from faith in the one God declining to idolatry, since previously all men were persevering in the worship of one God, and so such revelation was not necessary at that time. Likewise the fulness of revelation, regarding the Trinity and the Incarnation, was reserved to the time

---

*crementa temporum crevit scientia spiritualium patrum.*" Cf. II-II, q. 74, a. 6 obj. 1[um].

264 Eph. 3, 4-5.
265 Jn. 14, 26.

when the Son of God, having been made flesh, would found the Church, to be made fruitful by the conferral of multiple Sacraments, and to last until the end of time. Hence all are vain who expect after the time of the Apostles a new and more ample manifestation of supernatural things.

**27.—Comments**—The things that we have said formally relates to the manifestation of Divine truth inasmuch as it pertains to the *faith*: for if it be treated about revelation, to the extent that by it *we are governed in our actions*, it ought to be said that revelation was diversified not according to the passage of time, but according to the condition of the affairs; hence in each time there were not lacking some men having the spirit of the prophets, not actually for bringing forth a new doctrine of the faith, but for the direction of human acts: and thus in every time men were Divinely instructed concerning things to be done, according to what was expedient for the salvation of the elect; hence, as St. Jerome points out: "We read in the Acts of the Apostles that both Agabus and the four virgin daughters of Philipp prophesied";[266] and St. Augustine says that Theodosius Augustus "sent to John, whose abode was in the desert of Egypt—for he had learned that this servant of God (whose fame was spreading abroad) was endowed with the gift of prophecy—and from him he received an assurance of victory."[267]

**28.—The teaching of St. Thomas on the progress in matters of faith**—So that we may summarize the things which we have discussed up until this point, it can be said, with the Angelic Doctor, "As regards the substance of the articles of faith, they have not received any increase as time went on: since whatever those

---

266 *Exp. In Ep. ad Eph.*, c. 3. Cf. Acts 21, 9-10.
267 *City of God*, bk. 5, c. 26 (PL 41, 172).

who lived later have believed, was contained, albeit implicitly, in the faith of those Fathers who preceded them. But there was an increase in the number of articles believed explicitly, since to those who lived in later times some were known explicitly which were not known explicitly by those who lived before them."[268]

Since these things are so, what A. Loisy wrote ought to be completely rejected as foreign to the true and genuine concept of the dogmas of our faith: "The conceptions that the Church presents as revealed dogmas are not truths fallen from heaven, and preserved by religious traditions in the precise form in which they appeared... Though the dogmas may be Divine in origin and substance, they are human in structure and composition."[269]—Certainly, these words do away with the genuine concept of Catholic dogma, in that they give to be understood, not merely that its development is a human work, but that the development itself consists in the substantial transformation of our faith.

We conclude with St. Vincent of Lérins: "The intelligence, then, the knowledge, the wisdom, as well of individuals as of all, as well of one man as of the whole Church, ought, in the course of ages and centuries, to increase and make much and vigorous progress; but yet only in its own kind; that is to say, in the same doctrine, in the same sense, and in the same meaning."[270]

---

268 II-II, q. 1, a. 7.

269 *The Gospel and the Church* (New York, Scribner's Sons, 1912), pp. 210-211. "Les conceptions que l'Eglise présente comme des dogmes révélés ne sont pas des vérités tombées du ciel et gardées par la tradition religieuse dans la forme précise où elles ont paru d'abord... Que les dogmes soient divins par l'origine et la substance, ils sont humains de structure et de composition." (*L'Evangile et l'Eglise* (Paris, 1902), pp. 158-159).

270 *Commonitory*, c. 23, n. 54 (PL 50, 668).

# *Appendix II*

## Extracts from *De Stabilitate et Progressu Dogmatis*
by Cardinal Lepicier

### *Cardinal Newman's Treatment of the Development of Doctrine and his Profession of Faith*[271]

"[2.] Anxiety of the mind increases, however, because there are some who, and they are from among more distinguished men, have in fact published very good writings with the best intentions, yet others have attempted to make wrong use of them to their own ruin, while they take occasion from them of undermining the stability of Catholic dogma. Among whom ought to be reckoned Cardinal Newman, who in the many books published by him treats the subject of the increase and development of dogma not always with the method and manner which fully corresponds to objective truth.[272] To

---

271 *De Stabilitate et Progressu Dogmatis*, pp. 13-16.

272 The main book in which Cardinal Newman treats the question of the development of Catholic dogma is *An Essay on the Development of the Christian Doctrine*, which book he wrote while he was entering the Catholic religion. Yet when reading through which work, the reader ought to have before his eyes the preliminary declaration of the author (p. VIII, Ed., 1906: "Perhaps his (the author's) confidence in the truth and availableness of this view (of development) has sometimes led the author to be careless and over-liberal in his concessions to Protestants of the historical fact. If this be so anywhere, he begs the reader in such cases to understand him as speaking hypothetically, and in the sense of an argument *ad hominem* and *a fortiori*."—To this book ought to be

whom pardon will be willingly given, since he composed many things of this kind while he was still outside the fold of the Catholic Church, and by his personal study he earnestly tried to ascend to the bastion of truth; but those who having been born in the truth of the Church, can hardly be partakers of the same pardon who begin to desert it by new fictitious systems. And it is unimportant that they perceive that they have touched upon by their efforts those points of discipline which the previously praised Cardinal had come to, as though it would be turned to praise for them that this author travels the same way as they; for even if it were to be truly the same way, still it is travelled by them and by him for opposite reasons: for he was eagerly rising to the full possession of truth, but they miserably tumble down from the summit of truth to the darkness of error.

"Thus in order that it may be clear to everyone how the celebrated Cardinal, even though he had not familiarized himself sufficiently with Catholic dogma in many things, still he showed himself to be the most obsequious son of the Church, and he deeply abhorred those false conclusions which our Modernists attempt to extract from his writings, sometimes correctly, very often incorrectly, it will help to put before the eyes of the reader that splendid profession of faith which he has in his book, entitled, *Apologia pro vita sua*.— 'I believe the whole revealed dogma, as taught by the Apostles, as committed by the Apostles to the Church, and as declared by the Church to me. I receive it, as it is infallibly interpreted by the authority to whom it is thus committed, and (implicitly) as it shall be, in like manner, further interpreted by that same authority till the end

---

added: *An Essay in aid of a Grammar of Assent*; *A Lecture of the idea of a University*; *Apologia pro vita sua*, being a history of his religious opinions."

of time. I submit, moreover, to the universally received traditions of the Church, in which lies the matter of these new dogmatic definitions which are from time to time made, and which, in all times, are the clothing and illustration of the Catholic dogma as already defined. I submit myself to those other decisions of the Holy See, theological or not, through the organs which it has itself appointed, which, waiving the question of their infallibility, on the lowest ground come to me with a claim to be accepted and obeyed. Also I consider that, gradually, and in the course of ages, Catholic inquiry has taken certain definite shapes, and has thrown itself into the form of a science, with a method and a phraseology of its own, under the intellectual handling of great minds, such as St. Athanasius, St. Augustine and St. Thomas; and I feel no temptation at all to break in pieces the great legacy of thought thus committed to us for these latter days.'[273]—Notice how explicitly the man of great ability acknowledged the magisterium. Would that our Modernists, for those oversights which are found to be inaccurately stated in that well-known author, would make this egregious profession of faith as their own!

"Therefore the pious reader will give pardon, if in the course of these discussions, when we approvingly cite many opinions of this most eminent author, still at the same time we will take up not a few positions of the same man to be opposed: certainly, this will only be done for the sake of the truth, which alone all ought to serve, keeping at any rate that respect which is due to such a great man."[274]

---

273 London, Longmans, 1891, p. 250.
274 The words of Pius X to the Most Reverend Bishop of Limerick, who had sent him the small work, *Cardinal Newman and the Encyclical Pascendi* (Longmans, 1908), ought to be noted here: "Truly in such a large quantity of literary works, whatever can

"**4. The way of immanence explained and refuted**—The first way consists in a certain propensity or promptitude towards receiving by faith those things which one has discovered that God has revealed, as though the external manifestation of God exactly corresponds to inward inclination of the mind and the innate desire of the heart: which inclination, therefore, because desire is the highest criterion, whereby it ultimately ought to be inferred that a revelation was in fact received.

"This way, although it may seem beautiful, and though it may especially please the Modernists,[276] it

be found which may seem foreign to the usual way of thinking of theologians, nothing can be found which would arouse suspicion about his own faith." [This more accurate and realistic translation is much less flattering than the one provided by Michael Davies in his book, *Lead Kindly Light* (The Life of John Henry Newman, Neumann Press, 2001): "Truly, there is something about such a large quantity of work and his long hours of labour lasting far into the night that seems foreign to the usual way of theologians: nothing can be found to bring any suspicion about his faith." The original Latin is as follows: *Profecto in tanta lucubrationum eius copia quidpiam reperiri potest, quod ab usitata theologorum ratione alienum videatur: nihil potest, quod de ipsius fide suspicionem afferat.* (Letter *Tuum illud opusculum*, March 10, 1908). Although *lucubrationum* does indeed mean "nocturnal studies" in the literal sense of the word, this meaning does here not fit the context. For then it would be inferred that most theologians never study at night as does the Cardinal, who is then heroic for studying at night and consequently the pope needs to proclaim such heroicity for merely doing so! Also, by expansively translating *lucubrationum* (literally, "lucubrations") as "long hours of labour lasting far into the night," would seem to indicate a strong bias favorable to the Cardinal either by the translator, Mr. Davies, or more probably by both.]

275 *De Stabilitate*, pp. 17-18.

276 Among whom the atheistic author, Marecel Hérbert, deserves special mention, who in his work, *L'evolution de la foi*

will be easily detected by anyone that it suffers from an intrinsic error, as soon as he notices that it rests upon this false principle, namely that knowledge of both chief natural and supernatural truths is naturally innate to us. Certainly, since it is man's condition that he possesses no knowledge regarding external things which he has not drawn from the application of the senses by his own labor, it is completely groundless to have recourse to the knowing subject's intrinsic conscience, whether from ancient or of more recent authors, for having firm and certain knowledge of revealed truths. Of course such a way, since it lacks all foundation of truth, ought to be deemed simply erroneous and at the same time most dangerous, since faith is bound to perish in one who does not perceive in himself such an inclination to receiving the sentiments of revelation.

"To this position, which more recently authors seem to have taken from Plato, and which they are accustomed to call by the name of *imminence*,[277] pertains that

---

*catholique* (Paris, Alcan, 1905), tries to explain the development of the faith by the innate religious sense in man, to the point to being a theological system, which nevertheless ought to so make way for a purer form of religion (*evolution d'une nouvelle mentalité*, p. 210). And yet how pernicious this method of reasoning is, the author proves by his own example, who by force of his own principles was brought to the point that he denied the very existence of God distinct from the world.

277 Our Most Holy Father, Pius X, very recently laid bare the very subtle construction of the system of *Immanence* in his encyclical, *Pascendi*. Let the prudent reader judge how erroneous an author recently wrote ("Some Recent Books on Catholic Theology," in the *American Journal of Theology* (Jan. 1906, p. 179)): "It is with the apologetic of Duns Scotus and Cardinal Newman that the Catholic writer today meets the agnostic position [set down by the author of *Évolution de la joi catholique*,] and brings the good old doctrine of 'immanence' to the help of intellectualism in his campaign against unbelief."

which concerning our knowledge of things Kant asserted when he distinguished phenomena from noumena in this, that the former in fact represents a subjective perception, but the latter represents the very objective reality itself, and the former can really be perceived by us, but nowise the latter, even if we be brought by a blind instinct to attributing a real existence to things whose phenomena we perceive."

## His Ambiguous Position about Our Knowledge of God's Existence[278]

"The above above-praised Cardinal Newman is said to have reckoned nowise differently since, for proving God's existence, he appeals to the testimony of conscience. For he says, 'As from a multitude of instinctive perceptions, acting in particular instances, of something beyond the senses, we generalize the notion of an external world, and then picture that world in and according to those particular phenomena from which we started, so from the preceptive power which identifies the intimations of conscience with the reverberations or echoes (so to say) of an external admonition, we proceed on to the notion of a Supreme Ruler and Judge, and then again we image Him and His attributes in those recurring intimations, out of which, as mental phenomena, our recognition of His existence was originally gained."[279] From which words this author concludes that the knowledge of the turpitude of some actions is so founded upon God's pro-

---

278 *De Stabilitate*, pp. 18-20.

279 *An Essay in Aid of a Grammar of Assent*, "Belief in one God," p. 101, London, 1870. Cf. Mich. Cronin, D. D., *The Science of Ethics*, vol. 1, p. 476. Dublin, 1909. This author when citing the aforesaid words, instead of "instinctive" perceptions, has "intuitive" perceptions.

hibition itself, impressed in us along with God's existence, that even if that knowledge were to be lost, still this can never be erased.[280]

"Against which it ought to be noticed, that the dictate of conscience is a testimony that God exists and that He forbade certain actions, or that the conscience can be called God's voice, indeed bears witness that some order of morality whereby we are commanded both to do good and to avoid evil: but that this order of morality will be actually founded upon the very wisdom, justice, sanctity of a first being subsisting in himself and really distinct from the whole universe of things, Whom we call God, one knows from elsewhere than from the conscience itself. Hence also we sufficiently apprehend the deformity of our acts antecedently to the knowledge of God's actual precept or prohibition; moreover, if *per impossibile* some region were given, in which the notion of God's existence, I do not speak of His attributes, was absent, still in the recesses of the human heart the voice of conscience would resound now tormenting or torturing, now reprehending or stimulating.

"**5.—The true way is established for knowing revelation**—Which things since they are so, to someone asking how the voice of conscience bears witness that God exists and has spoken to men, the answer will be given, that this happens both negatively and positively: negatively indeed, insofar as nothing is in the conscience which is opposed to revelation; but positively, insofar as from the very acts of conscience reflexively perceived by reason, one can rise up to a first cause,

---

280 "In this special feeling, which follows on the commission of what we call right and wrong, lie the materials for the real apprehension of a Divine Sovereign and Judge... Though I lost my sense of (the) moral deformity (of my acts), I should not therefore lose my sense that they were forbidden to me." (*Ibid.*, pp. 102-103).

which is God, whose moral precepts, at the same time
that they are known, are perceived to very much agree
with the natural inclination of conscience."

### *His False Supposition that the Assent of Faith Rests Upon an Accumulation of Probabilities*[281]

**"9.—The assent of faith does not rest upon mere
probabilities**—From these things it ought to be deduced that Cardinal Newman did not come as close to
the truth, when he wrote that he preferred, in estab-
lishing the fact of the existence of the Christian religion,
to rely on an accumulation of probabilities, rather than
to draw out that fact from logical demonstrations: as
though any kind of proofs whatsoever, with which one
can be persuaded to accepting revelation, deviates from
the straight course of science.[282]

---

281 *De Stabilitate,* pp. 24-26.

282 It seems good to cite the very words whereby Cardinal
Newman opens his mind: "It is pleasant to my own feelings to
follow a theological writer, such as Amort, who has dedicated to
the great Pope Benedict XIV, what he calls 'a new, modest, and
easy way of demonstrating the Catholic Religion.' In this work he
adopts the argument merely of the GREATER PROBABILITY; I
prefer to rely on that of an ACCUMULATION of various probabilities; but we both hold (that is, I hold with him), that from probabilities we may construct legitimate proof, sufficient for certitude.
I follow him in holding, that since a Good Providence watches over
us, he blesses such means of argument as it has pleased Him to
give us, in the nature of man and of the world, if we use them duly
for those ends for which He has given them; and that, as in mathematics we are justified by the dictate of nature in withholding our
assent from a conclusion of which we have not yet a strict logical
demonstration, so by the like dictate we are not justified, in the
case of concrete reasoning and especially of religious inquiry, in
waiting till such logical demonstration is ours, but on the contrary
are bound in conscience to see truth and to look for certainty by
modes of proof, which, when reduced to the shape of formal propo-

"'For no historical fact do so great and so much evidence support the arguments, as are at hand for the fact of the existence of Christian revelation: hence concerning this matter the highest certitude is found, at least a moral certitude, namely such as can be reasonably desired in matters of this kind. Wherefore the following proposition was deservedly condemned by Pius X: 'The assent of faith ultimately depends on an accumulation of probabilities.'"[283]

"Now regarding Cardinal Newman, perhaps he hit the nail on the head who said that he meant by the word probability what we mean by moral certitude: which can be shown to be the case from the fact that he compares that kind of argumentation, which we can have concerning revealed religion, to the kind of argumentation whereby everyone proves his own birth and future death.[284]

---

sition, fail to satisfy the severer requisition of science." (*An Essay in aid of a Grammar of Assent*, "Revealed Religion," London, 1870, pp. 406-407).

283 This is proposition 25 in the decree, *Lamentabile*, of July 3, 1907 (Dz. 2025).

284 "For me it is more congenial to my own judgment to attempt to prove Christianity in the same informal way in which I can prove for certain that I have been born into this world, and that I shall die out of it." (*Ibid.*) And afterwards he explicitly wrote: "The very idea of Christianity in its profession and history is... a *Revelatio revelata*: it is a definite message from God to man distinctly conveyed by His chosen instruments, and to be received as such a message; and therefore to be positively acknowledged, embraced, and maintained as true, on the ground of its being divine, not as true on intrinsic grounds, not as probably true, or partially true, but as absolutely certain knowledge, certain in a sense in which nothing else can be certain, because it comes from Him Who neither can deceive or be deceived." (pp. 381-382).

"Still whatever may be the case, the most eminent author wrongly cites the authority of Eusebius Amort,[285] since this writer tried to establish something completely different, who doubtlessly was arguing as follows: The moral certitude of the true Church founded namely on the ordinary motives of credibility, can evade metaphysics by reflection, namely by noticing God's providence, which can absolutely never fail, especially in matters of religion; hence that motive of credibility, considered under this light, ought then to be said to have an infallible certitude.—But, if someone considers the matter more closely, he will unmistakably detect that this kind of argumentation suffers from the fault which is called begging the principles, since arguing in this way one is forced to suppose the existence of some religion revealed by God, which is precisely that which is being questioned."

### He Ought Not to be Called a Father of the Church[286]

"Likewise, every Catholic ought to abstain from some men's exaggerated manner of speech, calling Cardinal Newman the most recent Father of the Church."

### He shows a false conception of Scholasticism[287]

"Let the prudent reader judge how truly false is the notion of Scholasticism which Cardinal Newman exhibited when he wrote, "In Christianity, opinion, while

---

285 *Ethica Cristiana*, quoted by Cardinal Newman, work cited, p. 407.

286 *De Stabilitate,* p. 153.

287 *Ibid.,* p. 159.

a raw material, is called philosophy or scholasticism; when it is rejected, it is called heresy."

## He was not sufficiently educated in Scholastic doctrine[288]

"History is witness that every great genius, who ever enlightened the teachings of the Church by his preaching, discourses or writings, were debtors for his progress to the daily and diligent study of sacred doctrine, attained either under the best Catholic teachers or in their sound works: for in this way we know Saint Thomas even from his childhood was exercised in this most salutary study under learned teachers, which history also relates about the very distinguished Bossuet: on the contrary, the things which we find worthy of reprehension in the works of Cardinal Newman ought to be ascribed to his lack of scholastic education, certainly without the fault of that author, since he earnestly entered the Catholic Church."

## He Falsely Differentiates between the Fathers and the Scholastic Teachers[289]

"That the study of the scholastic teachers ought not to be disjoined from the study of the Fathers in him who desires to make true progress in the doctrine of the faith follows from those things which we have taught above about the scholastic method, which we said attains the same thing, but by the scientific and precise method, which the Fathers solved by prayer: hence the difference between the Fathers and the scholastics is not well assigned, as though the writings of the former were

288 *Ibid.*, p. 187.
289 *Ibid.*, p. 282.

informed with a life, which [is lacking] in the scientific investigations of the latter. Wherefore it nowise pleases what Cardinal Newman wrote long ago: 'All theological definitions come short of concrete life. Science is not devotion or literature. If the Fathers are not cold, and the Schoolmen are, this is because the former write in their own persons, and the latter as theologians or disputants. St. Athanasius or St. Augustine has a life, which a system of theology has not. Yet dogmatic theology has its importance notwithstanding.'[290] Certainly the supposition ought to be denied, that a living exposition of the faith can certainly be had, to which scholastic doctrine has not supplied the elements of the truth."

## His Erroneous Position concerning Inspiration[291]

"From the fact that the authors of the Sacred Scripture are instruments of God, it follows that everything that they wrote ought to be attributed to God as its author, and hence not only the ideas, but also the words are inspired.—Due to the fact that this truly most certain doctrine has been abandoned, particularly on account of the authority of Cardinal Newman, who maintained only the inspiration of ideas, great confusion has been brought into the schools, which nevertheless Leo XIII took away, having published the famous encyclical, *Providentissimus Deus* (Nov. 18, 1899), in which he says: 'For, by supernatural power He so roused and moved them to write, He stood so near them, that they rightly grasped in mind all those things, and those only, which He Himself ordered, and willed faithfully to write them down, and expressed them properly with infallible

---

290 *Lectures on Justification*, 1874, p. 31.
291 *De Stabilitate*, p. 302.

truth; otherwise, He Himself would not be the author of all Sacred Scripture.'[292]

"The foundation of the celebrated Cardinal's error is laid in the fact that he distinguishes in the Sacred Books that which is from God from that which is from man, as though it could not be the same thing from both, namely all from God, as the primary and principle cause, and all from man as the instrumental cause: for so the Cardinal wrote: 'By reason of the difficulty of always drawing the line between what is human and what is divine, (the Word of God) cannot be put on the level of other books,' etc."[293]

## His Erroneous Position concerning False Philosophy[294]

"**12.—One ought to assiduously guard against false philosophy**—Lest anyone suppose that every training, even one which is based upon false philosophy, helps for increasing the knowledge of the doctrine of the faith, here we earnestly caution that from that training alone, which is drawn from the principles of true and genuine philosophy, can true progress in the knowledge of sacred doctrine be obtained. For since there is not two but one source of natural truth and supernatural truth, for just as it is impossible that there would be a contradiction between science and the faith, so it is necessary that through errors about natural truths man is hindered from a fuller knowledge of the truths of the

---

292 Dz. 1952.

293 "What is of obligation for a Catholic to believe concerning the inspiration of the Canonical Scriptures." Being a Postscript to an article in the February N.º of the *XIX<sup>th</sup> Century Review*, in answer to Professor Healy, London, Burns and Oates.

294 *De Stabilitate,* pp. 349-350.

Catholic faith;[295] but because scholastic philosophy, which is the Stagirite's [Aristotle's], is the only true philosophy, no philosophical system effectively serves as a handmaid to sacred theology except one which is informed with scholastic doctrine.

"Wherefore it always was the heartfelt wish of the Church to provide that young men called unto the hope of receiving Orders, be instructed especially in scholastic philosophy, which is the open door to sacred theology; and very recently the Supreme Pontiff Pius X wrote: 'So far as studies are concerned, it is Our will and We hereby explicitly ordain that the Scholastic philosophy be considered as the basis of sacred studies... And what is of capital importance in prescribing that Scholastic philosophy is to be followed, We have in mind particularly the philosophy which has been transmitted to us by St. Thomas Aquinas... We admonish teachers to keep this religiously in mind, that disregarding Aquinas, especially in matters of metaphysics, even slightly cannot be done without great harm.'[296]

"Therefore here students have, and teachers have, from the highest teacher of the Church, who is Christ's vicar, to whom belongs the duty of safeguarding the deposit of faith, a most clearly indicated guide, whom they ought to follow in the study of sacred things: which solemn admonition has in fact been given as many times as this subject has been addressed by the Roman Pontiffs; wherefore we reckon that he by no means whatsoever deviates from the truth who would say that this

295 Hence the following words of Cardinal Newman nowise ought to be approved: 'The same man may run through various philosophies or beliefs, which are in themselves irreconcilable, without inconstancy, since in him they may be nothing more than accidental instruments or expressions of what he is inwardly from first to last." (*An Essay on the Development*, etc., pp. 174-175)

296 Ep. Encycl. *Pascendi*, Sept. 8, 1907.

is an object of ecclesiastical faith; and hence we cannot understand how not a few men, despising or neglecting this admonition, dare to call themselves Catholics."